Birthday book from
Hilary Breeze
March 31, 1987

The Grumpy Prophet

and 22 Other Bible Stories to Read and Tell

by John Calvin Reid

illustrated by Kathryn Hutton

STANDARD PUBLISHING
Cincinnati, Ohio   3370

DEDICATION

To my life-partner, Charlotte—
always supportive, encouraging, inspiring,
and loving.

Library of Congress Cataloging-in-Publication Data

Reid, John Calvin, 1901-
  The grumpy prophet and 22 other Bible stories to read and tell.

  Summary: A collection of retold Bible stories from the Old and New
Testaments, beginning with the building of Solomon's temple and ending with
some of the parables of Jesus. Each story includes an introduction, a brief
prayer, and discussion questions.
  1. Bible stories, English.   [1. Bible stories]
I. Hutton, Kathryn, ill.   II. Title.   III. Title:
Grumpy prophet and twenty-two other Bible stories to read and tell.
BS551.2.R39   1968   220.9'505   86-6028
ISBN 0-87239-917-6

PREFACE

The Bible stories in this book are a continuation of my first book, *30 Favorite Bible Stories.* The first is a father and son story featuring David and Solomon. This and the other stories that follow from the Old Testament are arranged in chronological order.

For each story there is a lead-in introduction and a brief prayer at the end, followed by discussion questions—underscoring the fact that these stories are intended to instruct and inspire the children who read or hear them, as well as to hold their interest.

The Gospel stories are about several friends of Jesus whose lives were dramatically changed as they came to know Him.

In the Parable stories, I've made an effort to apply several of Jesus' parables in such a way as to make clear what they should mean to us today, not forgetting the little girl's definition of a parable, "an earthly story with a heavenly meaning."

To readers one and all may I say

The stories I like best
I have rewritten for you;
I hope you will love them
As I still do.

—John Calvin Reid

CONTENTS

CHAPTER ONE

FATHER AND SON PARTNERS

This Bible story is about the first real temple the people of Israel had. It was built of stone and iron and wood—built because a father and son dreamed and planned and worked together to make it all come true.

As you read it, remember that your church building, too, was once the dream of those who loved God and wanted to honor Him by creating a beautiful place to worship Him.

* * * * * * *

The Bible does not tell us just when David, the king of Israel, and Solomon, his son, first talked together about building a temple in Jerusalem. But it does tell us that it was a project that they planned together. So we can well imagine that when Solomon was still a little boy, his favorite toy may have been a set of blocks, given to him by his father, David. One day, as he played with his blocks, he might have called to David, who was sitting close by, and said, "Look, Father! See what I am building."

"Yes, Son, I see," said David, as he came over to where Solomon was. "What is it? Wait, let me guess. A fort?"

"No, not a fort."

"A house?"

"No, but you are getting close."

"A palace?"

"No, something finer than a palace."

"I give up. What could be finer than a palace?"

"A temple," said Solomon, "a house for God."

"Yes, of course," said David. "You are right! God's house should be finer than a king's palace."

"Then, Father, why isn't it?" Solomon asked.

"What do you mean?" asked David.

"The house we have for God here in Jerusalem," answered Solomon, "is not nearly as fine as our palace. It is not even built of wood and stone, but of canvas. It's just a big tent. I think God's house should be the most beautiful house of all."

"You are so right, my son," agreed David. "I have been thinking about that for a long time."

Several years later, when Solomon was older and able to understand, David told him how he had been planning for a long time to build a temple in Jerusalem. He explained how he had been busy for several years getting the materials ready—lumber and iron and brass, gold and silver and precious stones. Then he showed Solomon a drawing of the temple he had in mind.

"I like it," Solomon said, as they looked at it together. "I am so glad you are going to build it."

"But I am not going to build it," David answered. "God has revealed to me that you will be the next king after me, and that it is His plan for you to build the temple. All the materials I have col-

lected and this drawing will all be yours.

"Be strong and very brave, and never be discouraged. God himself will guide and help you. I pray that He will give you wisdom and strength to finish building His temple and also to keep His commandments and to be a good king."

Solomon never forgot those words of his father, and, when he became king some years later, one of the first things he did was to begin building the temple. He was careful to hire the most skillful and artistic workmen he could find. Also he used only the very best of materials.

It took seven years to build it. When it was finished it was so wonderful that people came from far and near to see it and to worship God in it.

On the day it was dedicated, Solomon stood in front of the altar on a platform five feet high and, as the people bowed their heads, he prayed:

"O God, how great You are! So great that all the sky around and above is not big enough for You to live in! How much less this house we have built for Your home! But let Your eyes be upon this place day and night, and when Your people pray to You here, hear their prayer and forgive their sins."

Then he added:

"And blessed be the God of Israel who put it into the heart of David my father to build a house to the glory and the honor of Your name, and who helped me to complete my father's dream."

When Solomon had finished his prayer, all of the people said, "Amen."

Then there was a special song:

"How lovely is Thy dwelling place,
O Lord of hosts;
A day in Thy courts is better

Than a thousand elsewhere;
Blessed are those who dwell in Thy house,
Ever singing Thy praise" (from Psalm 84).

Thus the service ended.

As you may know, for four hundred years, until Jerusalem was destroyed by an army from Babylon, Solomon's temple, as it was called, was the center of worship for the people of Israel.

While we know God is everywhere and can be worshiped anywhere, we can be sure that He was greatly pleased with David and Solomon. As father and son, they had worked together with much understanding to create a beautiful place for God's people to come together to praise Him.

Prayer: Dear God, teach me how to work together with other people, especially with the members of my family.

And give me an appreciation for the beautiful things others have dreamed and created with the talents You gave them. Then show me things I can do to make Your world still more beautiful. In Jesus' name, amen.

Questions for Discussion

1. What was the secret David told to Solomon?
2. What was David's part in building the temple?
3. What was Solomon's part?
4. Tell what happened on the day the temple was dedicated.
5. What are some things that you and your father or mother do as partners?

CHAPTER TWO

WHOSE BABY?

Perhaps you know the Greek fable about King Midas.

Midas had done a good deed. And Bacchus, one of the Greek gods, rewarded him by promising, "Whatever you wish, you may have."

Now, as a child, Midas had been very poor, so he said to Bacchus, "I want to be rich, so my wish is that everything I touch may turn to gold."

Bacchus knew Midas had made a very foolish choice, but he gave him what he asked for.

At first, Midas was thrilled! He picked up a stick, a stone, an apple—each turned to gold in his hand! Arriving home, he ordered his servants to prepare a big banquet. But when he sat down to enjoy the feast, the bread he picked up turned to gold and broke his teeth when he tried to bite it. The wine in his glass became molten metal when he tried to drink it.

To keep from starving, he begged Bacchus to deliver him from the curse which he thought would be a blessing. He was told to go and bathe in the river Pactolus. By doing that, he finally washed away his sin of greed and learned that there are other things in life more important than money.

This Bible story is about a real king who was given a choice very much like the one that was offered to Midas. But his wish was ever so much wiser than the wish made by King Midas.

* * * * * * *

After David's death, the next king of Israel was his son, Solomon. At the beginning of his reign, Solomon was a very good king.

One night soon after he became king, God came to him in a dream and asked, "What would you like for me to give you?"

Solomon's answer was a prayer. "O Lord," he said, "my father, David, was a wise and good king. Compared to him, I feel like a little child. But You have made me king in his place and Your people have become a great nation. I am not wise enough to rule over them.

"So give me, I pray, a wise and understanding heart to know the difference between right and wrong so I may be able to rule with justice and fairness to all."

God was pleased with this prayer. It showed that Solomon was thinking more of his duty to his people than of his own fame or happiness. And God said, "You might have asked to be rich or to have a long life or to be successful in war, but instead you have asked for wisdom. So I will give you what you have asked." And

God kept His promise and gave Solomon wisdom and understanding.

One of the many times that Solomon used his wisdom was when he listened to an argument between two women.

One said, "Your Majesty, this woman and I live in the same house. That baby in her arms is mine. Her baby died in the night, and while I was asleep, she stole my baby from my side and put her dead baby in my bed. I did not know what she had done until I woke up this morning and found her dead baby beside me."

"No, no!" said the other woman. "The living baby is mine. The dead baby is hers."

"She is telling a lie!" exclaimed the first woman. "The dead baby belongs to her. She stole my baby. Make her give it back!"

Solomon knew, of course, that one of the women was telling a lie. So he said to himself, "The woman that loves the living baby most is the real mother. I will put them to a test."

"Bring me the baby," he said to the woman who held him. Then Solomon handed the baby to a soldier standing by his throne and called to another soldier to bring him a sword. The two women stepped back, shocked at what the king was about to do.

"Now," said Solomon, "both of you claim the living baby. I will divide him, then each one of you will have half."

Of course, Solomon had no idea of hurting the baby. He was only playacting or pretending, to see what the two women would do.

He had hardly finished speaking when one of the women rushed forward and threw herself at his feet. "No, no Your Majesty! Do not harm the baby. Give him to the other woman and let her keep him, but do not touch him with your sword."

"This is the baby's mother," said Solomon, as he took her by the hand and lifted her up. "She is the one who really loves him. Give the baby to her. Take the other woman away."

And all who heard the story were amazed at the wisdom of Solomon. He was honored far and wide as one of the wisest kings that ever lived.

Prayer: Dear God, like Solomon, I ask that You give me the wisdom to know the difference between right and wrong.

Then with Your help, may I have the courage always to do what I know is right and to refuse to do what I know is wrong. In Jesus' name, amen.

Questions for Discussion

1. What could Solomon have asked for other than wisdom?
2. Why was his prayer a good one?
3. What were the two mothers arguing about?
4. How did Solomon show his wisdom?
5. If God made you the same offer he made to Solomon, what would you ask for?

CHAPTER THREE

ONE AGAINST FOUR HUNDRED AND FIFTY

What is your favorite sport? Basketball? Baseball? Soccer?

In all of these sports, for the game to be interesting and fair, opposing teams must have the same number of players. In basketball, it is five against five; in baseball, nine against nine; in soccer, eleven against eleven. Right?

Well, what would you think of a game or contest in which the setup was 1 against 450? That is what this Bible story is all about.

* * * * * * *

"There you are, you troublemaker! Where have you been hiding for the last three years?"

It was Ahab, king of the nation of Israel who was speaking, and he was speaking to Elijah, one of Israel's most famous and courageous prophets.

"It is not I who am making trouble, but you!" Elijah shot back. "You and Jezebel, your wife, have disobeyed the commandments of Jehovah, the God of Israel, by turning away from Him and worshiping Baal, the idol god of the Sidonians. That is why there has been no rain upon the land for three years. However, Jehovah is now about to send rain.

"But first there is something you must do," Elijah continued. "Gather the nation to Mt. Carmel. Summon also the 450 prophets of Baal and there on Mt. Carmel we will see who has the power to bring rain, Baal or Jehovah."

Jezebel was a very wicked and violent queen. She was the daughter of the king of Sidon and was determined to kill all the prophets of Israel, including Elijah. (That explains why Elijah had been hiding for three years.) She wanted to make Baal the god of Israel, as well as of her people, the Sidonians.

But now, Elijah had come out from hiding and was about to expose the foolishness of Baal worship. Ahab did summon his people to Mt. Carmel as Elijah had asked him to do. The 450 prophets of Baal were there too. All were wondering what Elijah was going to do. They did not have long to wait!

Facing Ahab, but addressing the people, too, Elijah said, "How long will you go limping from one side to the other? If Jehovah is the real God, follow Him. But if Baal is the real God, follow Him."

As the people listened spellbound, he continued, "Look, Baal's prophets are here, 450 in number, while I am the only prophet of Jehovah present. Let them prepare a bull to sacrifice upon their altar, and I will prepare one to sacrifice upon Jehovah's altar. Neither of us will set fire to the wood under the sacrifice, but we will pray—Baal's prophets will pray to Baal and I to Jehovah, the God of Israel—and the God who answers by sending fire, let Him be God!"

"Well-spoken," "Right on," "A fair test," the people shouted, and the con-

test was on. The prophets of Baal tried first. They prepared their altar, placed their sacrifice on it, then began to dance around it, shouting, "O Baal, hear us!"

But there was no answer and no fire!

Elijah mocked them. "Louder, cry louder," he said. "Perhaps Baal is away on a trip or resting in some quiet place or asleep. Surely, if he is a real God he will answer you. Don't give up, pray louder!" All day they shouted, but nothing happened!

Finally, Elijah said, "Stand back! Now it is my turn!"

Then, as the people and Baal's 450 prophets watched, he rebuilt the altar to Jehovah (it had been broken down during Ahab's reign) and placed the sacrifice he had prepared on it.

"Fill four jars with water and pour it on the altar," he said to the people, and they did. At his command they did it a second and third time. The water completely soaked the sacrifice and the wood under it and filled the ditch that Elijah had dug around the altar.

Then standing near the altar, Elijah lifted his eyes toward Heaven and prayed: "O Lord, Jehovah, let it now be known that You and You alone are the God of Your people Israel. Turn their hearts away from Baal and back to You, the one and only true God."

At that moment fire fell from Heaven burning the wood and the offering and the altar and licking up the water in the ditch. As the people saw what had happened, they fell on their knees and exclaimed, "Jehovah, He is God!"

A little later Elijah said to King Ahab, "Go to your chariot and hurry home, for a big rain is coming!" And before long there were flashes of lightning and the roll of thunder.

Ahab did hurry to his chariot and drove as fast as he could down the mountain and across the valley to the city of Jezreel. But faster than Ahab's horses was Elijah! So thrilled was he that God had sent the fire followed by the rain and that the people of Israel had repented from their sin of worshiping Baal and turned back to their God, Jehovah, that he ran in front of Ahab's chariot all the way to the gate of Jezreel.

But no wonder he was thrilled! In the contest on Mt. Carmel he had stood, 1 against 450 and had won! Or would it be more truthful to say, "He had stood up with God, 2 against 450, and the two had won?"

Prayer: Dear Heavenly Father, from this story may I learn that You plus one are always a winning combination. Then help me to remember that the important thing is not how many are on my side or how many are against me, but to make sure that I am always on Your side. In Jesus' name, amen.

Questions for Discussion

1. What did Elijah ask King Ahab to do?
2. What did Elijah say the test on Mt. Carmel would prove?
3. While the prophets of Baal were praying, what did Elijah do?
4. Before Elijah prayed, what did he ask the people to do?
5. How was his prayer answered?
6. Discuss some of the ways we are tempted to "worship other gods" and what it means to "stand up" for Jesus.

CHAPTER FOUR

GOOD NEWS

What would you do if you were kidnapped? Well, I hope you never have to decide, because to be kidnapped would be a very frightening experience.

But in the Bible is the story of a little girl who was kidnapped, and—let us hear the whole story!

* * * * * * *

We do not know her name, the Bible does not tell us that. But we know from the Bible that this little girl was the daughter of Jewish parents and lived in the land of Israel many years ago. At the same time, in Samaria, one of the cities of Israel, lived a famous prophet by the name of Elisha.

The little girl knew about Elisha because her parents often talked of some of the wonderful things he did by the power of God. It was even reported that once, after praying to God, Elisha had brought back to life a little boy who had died.

Now in those days, to the north of the nation of Israel was a stronger nation called Syria. And sometimes a company of Syrian soldiers would ride down on their horses and kidnap some of the Jewish children, then carry them back to Syria and sell them as slaves. One day this happened to the little girl.

You can imagine how frightened she was as she was carried away. But, though she did not know it at the time, God was watching over her all the while

and getting her ready to do something very special—something the world would never forget.

Once the soldiers arrived back in Syria with the little girl, they sold her to an army officer whose name was Naaman, and he brought her to his wife to be her personal maid.

Now Naaman was a very brave and famous man in Syria. He was the commander in chief of the king's army, rich and popular. It might be said that he had everything for which his heart could wish except for one thing—he had leprosy.

In those days leprosy was a dreadful disease for which no cure was known. It was a disease in which the flesh, skin, and bones of one or more parts of the body would dry up and fall off or waste away.

So all the people, including the king, felt very sorry for Naaman, but no one knew anything to tell him to do.

That is, no one but the little servant girl! Although she was a slave in Naaman's home, and often homesick for her father and mother, she did not allow herself to become angry or sad. Before long she found herself feeling sorry for Naaman too.

One day she said to Naaman's wife, "Back in my country is a famous prophet, a man who does many wonderful things with God's help. I wish my master could go to him. He would heal

him from his leprosy."

That night Naaman's wife told him the good news. Naaman called the little servant girl in and asked her to tell him more about the prophet. This she did.

"Where does he live?" Naaman asked.

"In the city of Samaria," answered the little girl. "His name is Elisha."

So a few days later, Naaman, with several servants and rich gifts of gold and silver, started out for the land of Israel. When he arrived in Samaria, he asked where Elisha lived, then rode up to the front of his house.

But instead of coming out to meet him, Elisha sent a servant who said, "My master says for you to go wash in the river Jordan seven times, and you will be healed."

Now Naaman was not only famous and wealthy; he was also a very proud man. "Who does he think I am?" Naaman exploded. "I was sure he would come out, call upon his God, and wave his hand over the place where the leprosy is and heal me!" And Naaman drove away, boiling mad!

A little later, after he had cooled off, his servants said to him, "Sir, if the prophet had told you to do something hard, wouldn't you have done it? Then, why not go along when he asks you to do something simple and easy like bathing in the Jordan River?"

That was good advice, and Naaman took it. He drove down to the bank of the Jordan, took off his clothes, and dipped seven times into the water. And sure enough, the places on his body where the leprosy had been were instantly healed. His disease was gone!

Straight back to the prophet's house he rode. This time Elisha came out, and Naaman said to him, "Now I know that there is no God in all the world except your God. From now on, I will worship and serve the God of Israel, for He is the one true God."

Then Naaman offered Elisha the rich gifts of gold and silver he had brought. But Elisha refused them, saying, "It was God's power that healed you, not mine. Give Him the glory and go in peace."

So Naaman returned home feeling like a new man. A great burden had been lifted from his mind, and his heart was full of gratitude—gratitude to God and to Elisha, and, we may be sure, to the little servant girl too!

Prayer:

Dear God,
When things just seem to go wrong,
And I'm tempted to feel blue,
May I find someone in trouble,
And ask, what can I do?
In Jesus' name, amen.

Questions for Discussion

1. What did the little servant girl know about Elisha and how did she know it?
2. Tell what you know about Naaman.
3. When Naaman went to Elisha's home, what was he told to do?
4. Why did this make Naaman angry?
5. What made him change his mind?
6. What did Naaman say when he went back to Elisha's home after he had been healed?
7. Are there times when we should obey without asking questions? When?

CHAPTER FIVE

"GOD TO THE RESCUE!"

Have we trials and temptations?
Is there trouble anywhere?
We should never be discouraged,
Take it to the Lord in prayer.
— Joseph Scriven

Where have you heard these words? Did you recognize them as part of a hymn that is often sung in church worship services? These words teach us that when we are in real trouble, the wisest thing we can do is to talk to God about it.

This Bible story is about a king who, in an hour of deep distress, did "take it to the Lord in prayer."

* * * * * * *

Hezekiah's hand was shaking with fear as he read the letter from Sennacherib. In the letter, Sennacherib threatened to bring his mighty army and destroy Jerusalem, unless Hezekiah surrendered the city without a fight. Sennacherib was king of Assyria, the most powerful nation in the world at that time, and with his army had invaded the land of Judah. Judah was a very small nation, over which Hezekiah was king. Already Sennacherib had captured 45 towns in Judah. Now he was demanding that Hezekiah surrender the city of Jerusalem, too, including the king's palace and the magnificent temple Solomon had built some years earlier.

"You would be a fool," Sennacherib said in his letter, "to think that you and your pitiful little army can stand against my great army. Look at what I've already done."

Sennacherib listed seven nations he had conquered, then went on to say, "Were the gods of those nations able to deliver them? As you well know, I destroyed their cities and their gods. So, take my advice and surrender before I destroy Jerusalem and your God too."

It was those last words in Sennacherib's letter which made Hezekiah really angry. Straight to the temple he went, all the way up to the altar, and, laying the open letter on the altar, he began to pray:

"O Lord, Jehovah, You are the true God. Not of our nations only, but the God of all nations in the world. You are ruler over the whole earth. Look down from Heaven and see how Sennacherib is mocking You, the living God!

"True, the armies of Assyria have destroyed other nations and thrown their gods into the fire. But they were only idols made by men from wood and stone. That is why Sennacherib was able to destroy them. But you are the true God, and it is You whom we worship and trust. So now, O Lord, we ask You to save Your people from Sennacherib, that all nations in the world may know that You are the one and only true God."

In response to Hezekiah's prayer, God sent a special message to him through Isaiah, a well-known prophet of that time. This is the message he brought:

"This is the word God has spoken concerning Sennacherib, king of Assyria. I, the Lord God, am the ruler over all the earth, and I know and control everything Sennacherib does. I have heard his proud raging against me and his boasting about how he plans to destroy Jerusalem. So, I myself will defend the city in answer to your prayer and for the sake of my people.

"Sennacherib will not enter the city! He will not shoot even one arrow into it. But I will lead him back like a tamed animal to his own country. So, do not be afraid, Hezekiah. I have heard your prayer, and I myself will save Jerusalem!"

In the meantime, back where the Assyrian army was waiting, Sennecherib had issued an order to his generals: "Tomorrow, we march against Jerusalem!" But something happened that made him change his mind! That very night, God sent an angel into the camp where the Assyrian soldiers were sleeping, and the 185,000 soldiers did not wake up. The next morning they were dead men!

Stunned and frightened by that calamity, Sennacherib canceled his order to attack Jerusalem, and, with what soldiers were left, marched back in disgrace to Assyria. There, sometime later, he was murdered by two of his sons as he was praying to his idol god Nisroch. It was a sad but fitting end to a life devoted to cruelty and destruction. Sennacherib had reaped what he had sown! But the faith of King Hezekiah and Isaiah had been rewarded!

Prayer: Dear God, if I am ever afraid, may I follow the example of King Hezekiah and turn my fears over to You.
Lord, be with me day by day,
Guard me in my work and play;
Shield me by Your mighty arm,
Keep me safe from sin and harm;
Free my heart from every fear,
Knowing You are always near.
In Jesus' name, amen.

Questions for Discussion

1. Who was Hezekiah? Who was Sennacherib? Who was Isaiah?
2. What did the letter from Sennacherib to Hezekiah say?
3. How did Hezekiah feel when he read the letter?
4. What did Hezekiah say in his prayer?
5. What answer did God send to Hezekiah through the prophet Isaiah?
6. What does Hezekiah's example teach us that we should do about our fears?

CHAPTER SIX

STANDING UP FOR WHAT YOU BELIEVE

Do you know what the word "martyr" means? Well, once it meant simply "a witness"—one who stood for his faith and told others about it.

But during the early days of Christianity, there were Roman emperors who ordered Christians to be thrown to the lions or burned at the stake for claiming that Christ was their Lord. So many of them died rather than deny their faith, that the word "martyr" came to mean "one who gives his life for his faith."

This story is about three young men who were brave enough to tell a king that they would rather die than disobey God.

* * * * * * *

Shadrach, Meshach, and Abednego—three young men who loved God and kept His commandments—were appointed to high positions in Babylon by King Nebuchadnezzar. But that didn't keep them from trusting and obeying God.

Babylon was a heathen country where the people worshiped idols rather than the true God. King Nebuchadnezzar had set up a huge statue on the plain of Dura near his palace. This statue was made of gold, and was ninety feet high. One day the people of Babylon came together by order of the king to worship this new statue. When the king gave a signal, all became quiet and a herald proclaimed in a loud voice:

"You are commanded, all you people, whatever your race or country, when you hear the sound of horn, pipe, and every other kind of musical instrument, to fall to your knees and worship the golden statue that King Nebuchadnezzar has set up!"

Then, still louder he said, "And if anyone does not fall down and worship the statue he shall be thrown into a fiery furnace!"

When Shadrach, Meshach, and Abednego heard this, they looked at each other and shook their heads.

"We cannot do it," said Shadrach. "Remember the first commandment we were taught years ago, back in Canaan?"

"You shall have no other gods before me," said Meshach.

"And the second commandment says, 'You shall not make a graven image. You shall not bow down to statues nor serve them, for I am the Lord your God.'"

So, when the people fell on their knees before the golden statue at the sound of the music, Shadrach, Meshach, and Abednego stood straight up. They did not so much as bow their heads.

When Nebuchadnezzar was told this, he was very angry. He ordered them brought to the fiery furnace.

"Why have you disobeyed my command?" he asked.

"Because," they answered, "we worship the true God, and we have been taught that it is wrong to bow down before idols."

"And do you think your God is able to keep you from being burned up in the fiery furnace?" asked the king, pointing toward the roaring fire.

"We are sure He is able," they replied. "And we believe He will save us. But even if He allows us to die in the fire, we will not worship the gods of Babylon or bow before the golden statue!"

These brave words made the king furious! He ordered his servants to heat the furnace seven times hotter than ever before. Then Shadrach, Meshach, and Abednego were tied hand and foot and thrown into the fire.

As the king looked through the door into the furnace, he saw a strange sight.

"Look!" he cried, "was it not three men that we threw into the fire?"

"True," his servants answered, "the number was three."

"But I see *four,*" Nebuchadnezzar exclaimed, "and they are all walking through the fire, not hurt! And the fourth man looks like a son of God!"

Then the king came up closer and called:

"Shadrach, Meshach, and Abednego, servants of the Most High God, come out!"

When they did, the king and the people saw that not even their clothes or their hair had been scorched. There was no smell of fire at all.

You see, God had sent His angel to protect them from the fire. He was the fourth man the king had seen walking with them in the furnace.

"There is no god like your God," said Nebuchadnezzar. "From now on, you will be free to worship Him and Him only. No other God could have saved you."

Later, the king ordered that no one in his entire kingdom should ever say anything against the God of Shadrach, Meshach, and Abednego.

How wonderful it was that God sent His angel to guard them so that they came out of the fire unharmed. But also how wonderful that they had the courage to stand up for their faith and say to the king, "Even if our God does not save us, we will not worship or bow down before the golden statue you have set up!"

Prayer: Dear God, down through the years there have been many brave people who put You first and stood up for their faith, no matter what it cost them.

I thank You for their example, and pray that I may have the same kind of courage and always be true to my faith. In Jesus' name, amen.

Questions for Discussion

1. What two commandments would Shadrach, Meshach, and Abednego be breaking if they worshiped the golden statue? (See Exodus 20:1-4.)
2. What did they say to the king?
3. How did this make the king feel and what did he do?
4. What did the king see when he looked into the furnace?
5. What did Nebuchadnezzar say and do when they came out from the furnace unharmed?

CHAPTER SEVEN

HAND FROM OUTER SPACE

If someone went into your church building and stole the Bible from the pulpit, then later at a party tore out the pages and threw them in the fire—all the while making fun of God and laughing about the Bible—what would God think of such a person?

In this Bible story we hear what God thought about a king who did something very much like that.

****

Belshazzar was the king's name, and at the beginning of our story he was feeling great!

And why not? He had been the king of Babylonia for only a short time when (so a famous Greek historian tells us), his army had defeated and driven back the army of an enemy nation known as Media, which had tried to capture Babylon, his capital city. That victory called for a celebration!

So Belshazzar put on a big banquet. A thousand chief men in his kingdom were invited. During the evening, the banquet became a wild party.

Then the king did a very wicked and foolish thing. Calling to his servants he said, "The gold and silver goblets which my father Nebuchadnezzar took from the Jewish temple in Jerusalem, bring them to me."

Then those goblets, which up to this time had never been used except in services of worship in God's temple—Belshazzar filled them with wine, and he and his guests drank from them! And the people praised their idols of gold and silver, of iron and brass, of wood and stone. Holding the goblets high, they made fun of the God of Israel from whose temple the goblets had been taken.

Then, all of a sudden, the drinking and the making fun stopped! From outer space there floated into the palace the huge fingers of a man's hand! Belshazzar dropped his goblet, and he and his guests watched in stunned silence as the hand began writing on the wall right behind the king's head, just above the lamp, where everyone could see it.

When the hand finished writing, it floated up to the ceiling and out of the palace, but the strange writing was still there—four mysterious words in large letters: MENE, MENE, TEKEL, UPHARSIN.

Belshazzar's face was white! He called for his magicians and wise men to explain the writing.

"The man who can tell me what those words mean," he said, "shall be given a purple robe with a gold chain around his neck, and I will make him the third ruler in my kingdom!"

The wise men came, looked at the four strange words, and one after the other turned away. None of them could

tell what the words meant! Then Belshazzar was more frightened than ever!

Meanwhile, his mother, the former queen, heard what had happened and came into the banquet hall. Making her way to Belshazzar's table, she said, "I know a man who can tell you what the words mean."

Then she told him about Daniel: how he, a very young man at the time, had been brought over to Babylon from Jerusalem when the city was captured, and how he had been able to tell the meaning of dreams and solve problems for Belshazzar's father, the former king.

"Call him," she said. "He will tell you what the writing means."

So Belshazzar sent for Daniel, and when he came said to him, "I am told by my mother that you are one of the captives my father brought from Jerusalem, and that you served him with great wisdom and understanding in solving problems and explaining dreams."

"Whatever wisdom I have is God's gift," answered Daniel. "What can I do for your majesty?"

Belshazzar's hand was shaking as he pointed to the writing on the wall behind him, and his voice trembled as he said, "Those words! Tell me what they mean, and you will be clothed in a purple robe with a gold chain around your neck. Also, I will make you the third ruler in my kingdom."

"I will take no reward," replied Daniel, "because it is God who will reveal to me the meaning of the words."

Then Daniel showed his courage! Before he explained the writing, he reminded Belshazzar of how he had failed to be the kind of king God had expected him to be.

"God gave to your father, Nebuchadnezzar," he said, "a great kingdom and many honors. But instead of giving God the glory and being humble and grateful, he became proud and boastful. So he lost his mind for a time, and God took away his throne until he became humble and learned that God is the ruler over all the kingdoms of the world, and that it is He who decides who shall be king and who shall not."

Then looking straight into the face of the king, Daniel continued, "And you, although you knew all this, have made the same mistake your father made. You, too, have lifted yourself up in pride against the Lord of Heaven. On this very night you have made fun of Him by bringing to your table the sacred gold and silver goblets which were made to be used only in the temple. By drinking wine from them and praising your idols, which can neither see nor hear, you have insulted Him—the true God who gave you your life and your throne and all else that you call your own."

Then, pointing to the mysterious writing on the wall, Daniel added, "This God, whom you have made fun of tonight, it is His hand that has written those words, and this is their meaning:

"M E N E means "numbered"—God has counted the days of your reign, and your time is up!

"T E K E L means "weighed"—He has weighed you on the scales of His judgment and you are a miserable failure!

"U P H A R S I N means "divided"—your kingdom is about to fall, and will be given to the Medes and Persians!"

How did Belshazzar feel when Daniel finished speaking?

Perhaps he was angry and wanted to throw Daniel into prison but was afraid of what his guests might think.

Maybe he secretly admired Daniel's courage, even though he did not like what he had said.

It is even possible that he felt guilty and thought of trying to change his way of life but was too drunk to know how to begin.

More likely he and his guests felt so secure behind the high stone walls of Babylon that, after he had rewarded Daniel as he had promised, they laughed off his words of warning and went on with their drinking!

We do not know how Belshazzar felt. But we do know (from Greek history) that the army he had turned back did not return to Media, as Belshazzar had supposed, but marched back to Babylon, and even as Daniel was speaking, had already surrounded the city.

Led by a famous general by the name of Darius, the Medes again attacked, and this time they did capture Babylon.

So, on the very night that the strange words, "MENE, MENE, TEKEL, UP-HARSIN" appeared upon the wall of his palace, Belshazzar was killed.

What a shame that he did not learn from his father's experience that pride leads to destruction and a boastful spirit to a fall (see Proverbs 16:18).

Prayer: Dear God, keep me from ever being proud or boastful about what I have or can do. In the way I use the gifts and opportunities You give me, may I try always to please and honor You rather than myself. In Jesus' name, amen.

Questions for Discussion

1. What wicked, foolish thing did Belshazzar do?
2. What mysterious thing happened?
3. What reward did Belshazzar promise the man who could explain the meaning of the four words?
4. What did Daniel say to Belshazzar before he explained the writing on the wall?
5. What did the four words mean?
6. How do you think Daniel kept from feeling proud of his wisdom and greatness?
7. What should you do when you are tempted to boast?

CHAPTER EIGHT

THE LION TAMER

"Now I lay me down to sleep,
I pray the Lord my soul to keep;
God be with me through the night
And wake me with the morning light."

Did you learn that prayer when you were younger? And do you still say your prayers every night?

How about if you are spending the night with some of your friends or if you are away at camp, do you skip your prayers or say them silently in bed so no one will know you are praying?

This is a Bible story about Daniel and his courage. He had formed good prayer habits when he was young, and not even a king could make him change.

* * * * * * *

Just when Daniel began to pray he could not remember. His father and mother had taught him to love God and to talk with Him when he was a little boy.

Later, living far away from home and in a heathen country, he still made it his habit to pray three times every day. He was never too busy, even though at the time of this story he was one of three presidents who helped Darius, the new king, to rule his empire.

Daniel was such a good president that Darius planned to promote him and make him ruler over his entire kingdom. This made the two other presidents and certain government officers jealous, so they began plotting to get rid of him.

They watched everything he did but could find nothing to complain about to the king.

At last they decided upon this evil scheme. They went to the king and said, "O King Darius, may you live for ever! You are a great and noble ruler! You should be worshiped as a god!

"We feel you should make it a law that for thirty days no one shall offer a prayer or make a request to any man or god except to you.

"Also, Your Majesty, let it be stated that the law cannot be changed, and that if anyone disobeys, he shall be thrown into the den of lions."

Flattered at being told that he was like a god, and not knowing about the plot against Daniel, Darius ordered the law to be drawn up, and he signed it.

When Daniel heard about the new law, straight to his home he went and knelt down to pray. And he did not try to hide what he was doing! He prayed with his windows open toward Jerusalem.

Of course his enemies were watching, and when they saw him on his knees, they ran to the king, told him what they had seen, and demanded that Daniel be thrown into the den of lions.

Now the king admired Daniel so much that he was very sorry he had signed the law. But according to the custom of those times, the law could not be changed.

He told Daniel how sorry he was and added, "May your God, to whom you pray and whom you serve so faithfully, deliver you." Then Daniel was thrown into the den of lions and the door locked behind him.

That night the king could not sleep—he was so worried about Daniel! Very early the next morning, he hurried down to the lions' den and called, "Daniel, Daniel, has your God been able to save you from the lions?"

And Daniel answered, "Yes, Your Majesty. My God sent His angel to guard me. He shut the lions' mouths and they have not touched me. All night long I have been kept safe."

Then the king was glad and commanded that Daniel be let out. All who saw him were amazed because he had not been harmed at all.

Then Darius published a special decree and sent it to every part of his kingdom. It read, "Peace! I make a decree that in all my royal kingdom, men shall honor the God of Daniel because He is the living and true God."

The brave example of Daniel reminds us of two things. First of all, the God we read about in the Bible is the one true God. And second, it is very important for us to think about Him and talk with Him every day.

Prayer:

Dear God,
I thank You that when I kneel to pray,
You always hear what I have to say.
May I never be too busy to talk to You.
And never ashamed, if seen when I do.
I know You love me so very much,
So let us talk often, and never lose
   touch.
Amen.

Questions for Discussion

1. What were Daniel's prayer habits?
2. Describe the plot against him.
3. What did Daniel do when he heard about the new law?
4. What was done to him because he disobeyed the new law?
5. Why did the king hurry down to the den of lions the next morning, and what did he find?
6. What did he do after Daniel came out unharmed?
7. Have you ever been ashamed to pray?

CHAPTER NINE

BEAUTY PAGEANT

This Bible story is about a beauty pageant long ago in the land of Persia.

★ ★ ★ ★ ★ ★ ★

At the beginning, life was not easy for Esther. Her mother and father were among the Jews carried away to Babylon when Nebuchadnezzar captured Jerusalem around six hundred years before Jesus was born. (Remember this happened to Daniel and his three friends too.)

Probably Esther was born in Babylon. When she was very young, both her parents died. She missed them very much, but it was her good fortune to be adopted by a good cousin whose name was Mordecai. He took her into his home, and loved and cared for her as if she were his own daughter.

When she became a young woman, she was very beautiful. Then one day her big opportunity came—to enter a nationwide beauty contest. The reward: a crown and a palace! You see, Ahasuerus (also called Xerxes), the king of Persia (the same country that was once called Babylon), was looking for a queen. Following the advice of his lords, he sent a notice to his 127 governors for each to choose and send a beautiful girl to his palace. From these he himself would choose the new queen.

With Mordecai's approval, Esther entered the contest. But he warned her (since there was so much prejudice against Jews in Persia) to tell no one that she was a Jew. Mordecai loved her so much and was so concerned about her that he walked back and forth in front of the palace every day during the contest, hoping to hear how she was getting along.

You can imagine how thrilled he was when he heard that she had won and that the king himself had placed the royal crown on her head!

But, of course, Esther was even more thrilled! She had a crown, a palace, gorgeous clothes and jewelry, servants—everything for which her heart could wish!

But it wasn't long before she learned that being queen was not all pleasure.

The king's prime minister, Haman, was a very proud man—so proud that when he rode through the streets of the city on his fine horse, he expected all the people to bow down to him (as if he were some kind of god!), and all the people did, except one: Mordecai!

This made Haman furious! And when he found out that Mordecai was a Jew, his anger boiled!

"I'll get even," he said to himself, "and more!" So he decided not only that Mordecai must die, but all Jews in the whole kingdom of Persia!

The next morning he came to the king with a wicked lie and plot.

"Your Majesty," he said, "all through

your kingdom there is a certain group of people who are different from us and disloyal to you. They are against our government and do not keep our laws. I urge the king to order them to be destroyed. I have with me a decree which will take care of everything, if Your Majesty will just sign it."

Haman did not tell Ahasuerus that the people named in the decree were Jews. But when the king hesitated, he added, "And to express my gratitude, I am prepared to put into the king's treasury ten thousand talents of silver."

How money talks! The king signed immediately! He didn't even look at the decree—his mind was on the ten thousand talents of silver.

Mordecai was shocked when he heard about this decree, but what could he do? Nothing! Then he thought about Esther. Being the queen, she could do something!

So he sent her a message in which he told her about Haman's wicked plot and urged her to go to the king and plead with him to save her people.

But Esther was afraid to go.

"Everyone knows," she wrote back to Mordecai, "that there is a law in Persia that no one is allowed to go into the king's throne room without being called. If anyone goes in uninvited, he or she will be killed at once—unless the king holds out his golden scepter."

No wonder Esther was afraid, and Mordecai understood. But he did not want her to use her fear as an excuse for not doing her duty. So he sent back a second message, even more urgent than the first, "You must go to the king anyway." Then he added a question which really made Esther think, "Who

knows but that God made you queen for just such a time as this so you would be able to save your people?"

Deep down in her heart, Esther knew Mordecai was right. And although she was still afraid, she sent back a brave answer.

"Call together all the Jews in Shushan and pray for me. I and my maids will pray too. Then, after three days, I will go to the king, though I know it is against the law. Even if I die, it will be all right. I will have done my duty!"

So after three days of prayer, Esther put on her royal robe and her crown, and holding her head high, entered the throne room. The king rose and held out to her his golden scepter. Then Esther came forward and touched the top of the sceptor.

"Good morning, Queen Esther," said Ahasuerus, "what is your wish? It shall be given you, even to the half of my kingdom."

"If it pleases Your Majesty," Esther answered, "let the king and his prime minister come to my palace tomorrow evening to a special dinner which I will prepare in the king's honor."

"We will be pleased to come," the king replied.

All day long Haman was in high spirits because he alone of the king's ministers had been invited to the queen's dinner. But as he went out of the palace, he passed Mordecai, and again Mordecai did not bow down before him!

When he arrived home, he said to his wife, Zeresh, "Here I am, one of the richest men in Persia, prime minister to the king, and the only one of his ministers invited to the queen's dinner tomorrow night! But what does all of this mean

to me, as long as I see that Jew, Mordecai, standing in front of the palace and ignoring me?"

Then Zeresh said, "Come on! I'll tell you how to get rid of him! Have your servants build a gallows seventy-five feet high! Then, when you see the king tomorrow, ask him to order that Mordecai be hanged on it."

"Great idea!" said Haman. "I'll take care of it the first thing in the morning."

Now it so happened that Ahasuerus was not able to sleep that night, so he got up to read. And in one of his books he read for the first time about how Mordecai some years back had heard about a plot to murder the king and had reported it in time to save the king's life.

The next morning, when Haman arrived at the palace, Ahasuerus was thinking about Mordecai and what should be done to reward him for what he had done.

Haman was thinking about Mordecai, too, and what lie he could tell the king so he would order Mordecai to be hanged.

Ahasuerus spoke first.

"Good morning, Mr. Prime Minister. I need your advice about a very important matter. What shall be done for the man to whom the king wishes to show special honor?"

Haman said to himself, "There is no one the king would wish to honor more than his prime minister—he must mean me!"

So he answered, "For the man to whom the king wishes to show special honor, let him wear one of the king's royal robes and one of the king's crowns and ride the king's own horse. Then let one of the king's most noble princes lead the horse through the center of the

city, proclaiming, 'This is being done for the man whom the king is delighted to honor.'"

"Splendid!" exclaimed Ahasuerus. "You will be the noble prince to lead the horse. At the gate of the palace, ask for the man named Mordecai. He is the man to whom I wish to show special honor. Do for him as you have said."

Inside Haman was saying, "No! Oh no! This cannot be!" But he dared not refuse.

So, leading the king's horse, and with Mordecai riding behind clothed as a king, Haman walked through the city, proclaiming, "To this man the king is delighted to show special honor!"

That night, when he arrived for the queen's banquet, he was feeling very sorry for himself. But the worst was still to come!

Once he and the king were seated at the table, Ahasuerus said to Esther "Now what is the queen's wish. Again I say, even to the half of my kingdom it will be given you."

Then Esther told him about the cruel decree that called for the killing of the Jews through all the land of Persia. "They are my people," she added, "and it is my wish that no harm should come to them."

"Who is he that would dare do such a thing, and where is he?" Ahasuerus asked in anger.

"He is in this room, Your Majesty," Esther answered, "sitting right beside you! Your prime minister!"

Haman's face was white from fear and he was speechless. The king was very angry with Haman. So angry, in fact, that he ordered Haman to be hanged on the seventy-five foot high gallows that

Haman built for Mordecai!

How grateful Mordecai must have been to Esther! And how proud he was of her courage!

At the risk of her own life she had saved Mordecai's life and the life of her people, and had shown to all the world what a brave and unselfish queen she was! God had brought her to the throne for just such a time, and she had not failed Him.

Prayer:

Dear God,
So often I ask You to *give* me a blessing,
Which may mean I am thinking too much of *me;*
So, this time I ask You to *make me* a blessing,

And help me to think more of others and Thee.
Amen.

Questions for Discussion

1. Why did Esther live in the home of her cousin Mordecai?
2. How did she become the queen?
3. Who was Haman, and why did he plan to kill the Jews?
4. What was Mordecai's plan to save them?
5. Why was Esther afraid to go to the king?
6. Do you think Mordecai was proud of Esther? Give reasons.
7. Can God use you in some special way?

CHAPTER TEN

THE GRUMPY PROPHET

Do you remember the Walt Disney movie about Snow White and the Seven Dwarfs? The name of one of them, you will recall, was "Grumpy." How would you like that for a nickname?

Not at all, would you? Because the name "Grumpy" makes you think of someone who complains a lot and who doesn't like people. And you wouldn't want to be that kind of person, would you?

This Bible story is about a man whose real name was Jonah, but he might well have been nicknamed "Grumpy" because that was the kind of man he was!

* * * * * * *

Some of the most important people in the Old Testament were the prophets. So Jonah should have been pleased and honored when God singled him out and called him to be a prophet. But, as a matter of fact, he felt just the opposite! Why? Because he didn't want to do what God asked him to do.

"Go to the great city of Nineveh," God had said, "and preach to the people there. Tell them how displeased I am because of their sins, and call upon them to repent. Warn them that if they do not repent and turn from their sins, their city will be destroyed."

Why didn't Jonah want to deliver that message to Nineveh? Because he *wanted* the city to be *destroyed!* You see, the Assyrians who lived there had, for a long time, been the enemies of Jonah's own people, the Jews. Recently, they had defeated the Jews in war and had taken many of them to Nineveh as slaves. For this reason, Jonah really wanted Nineveh to be destroyed, not saved!

So, instead of doing what God told him to do, he went down to the sea, found a ship going to Tarshish, bought a ticket, and sailed away in the opposite direction from Nineveh.

But God sent a great storm upon the sea to teach Jonah that he could not run away from God. Huge waves pounded the ship until it was at the point of breaking to pieces. The sailors were frantic with fear! Then they questioned Jonah and found out who he was and that he was fleeing from God. "It is my fault that this great storm has come," Jonah said. "Throw me into the sea." So they threw him into the sea, and the storm quieted down.

But God did not let Jonah drown! He sent a great fish that swallowed Jonah whole without hurting him. For three days and nights, he was inside the fish. That gave him plenty of time to think about how foolish he had been. Also during that time, he did a lot of praying!

On the third day, God caused the great fish to cough Jonah up on dry land. Then, a second time, God said to him, "Jonah, I want you to go to Nineveh

and preach to the people there. Call upon them to repent and to forsake their sins."

This time Jonah did as God had commanded. Through the streets of the city, he went shouting: "Turn from your evil ways, or in forty days Nineveh will be destroyed!"

To Jonah's amazement, the people did repent. Even the king took off his royal robe and sat in ashes as a sign of his sorrow for his sins and called upon his people to turn to God and to pray that God would save them.

The people did as their king commanded, and God did forgive them.

At the end of the forty days, Jonah, seeing the city had not been destroyed, became very "grumpy" again. He went outside the walls and sat in the sun. He was very angry with God because He had not destroyed Nineveh.

As he continued pouting, the sun became hotter and hotter. Once again, God treated him better than he deserved. He caused a large vine with wide leaves to grow up over Jonah's head. That protected him from the heat of the sun and made him feel better for a little while.

But the next day, God caused the vine to wither. Jonah, feeling the hot rays of the sun on his head, became "grumpy" again and complained because the vine had died.

"Jonah," God said, "you should be ashamed of yourself! You wanted me to save the vine that sprang up and sheltered you from the heat of the sun, but you did not want me to save the 120,000 people of Nineveh. Should I not be concerned about them?"

God is a merciful, forgiving, and loving God. It is not His will that anyone should perish, but that everyone who calls upon the name of the Lord should be saved (Matthew 18:14, Romans 10:13).

Did Jonah finally learn this glorious truth about God? Or did he keep on being "grumpy?"

The Bible does not tell us. But let us hope that we have learned how loving and forgiving God is. Let us never forget it!

Prayer:

Dear Lord,
I'll go where You want me to go,
Over mountain, plain, or sea;
I'll say what You want me to say,
I'll be what You want me to be.
　　　　　—Charles H. Gabriel

I'll tell my friends how You love them,
That You want to save them, too;
Please help me never to be "grumpy,"
But each day more and more like You.
Amen.

Questions for Discussion

1. What did God ask Jonah to do?
2. Why did Jonah not want to do it?
3. What did Jonah do instead?
4. Then what did God do and why?
5. What did Jonah do while he was inside the great fish?
6. What did Jonah do after the fish coughed him up?
7. How should you treat people who are unkind or mistreat you?

CHAPTER ELEVEN

COMMENCEMENT DAY!

One day you will be graduating from high school and perhaps later from college. Those will be big days in your life, and what will they be called? *Commencement* Day!

Doesn't that seem strange? Shouldn't it be "Finishment Day" or "Achievement Day?" The words *finished* and *achievement* point to the past. They remind you of what you *have already done,* while the word "commencement" points to the future. It reminds you that your life has really just begun and challenges you to "forget the things that are behind and to press on toward the goal" that God has in mind for you.

This Bible story is about "Commencement Day" in the life of Jesus.

* * * * * * *

His name was John, but he looked more like a wild man than a preacher. His hair was long and shaggy, and so was his beard. His coat or robe was woven from the coarse hair that grows on the back of a camel. Around his waist he wore a wide leather belt.

He lived out in a desert place where food was hard to find. So, when he was hungry, he ate insects called locusts and honey which wild bees stored in hollow trees or rocky hillsides. He had no church building or synagogue in which to preach, so he preached in the open country beside the bank of a stream called the Jordan River.

And, strange as it may seem, great crowds from far and near came to hear him—some even from the city of Jerusalem, twenty miles away.

"God's day of judgment is coming!" he shouted. "But if you turn away from your sins and are baptized, God will forgive you." Those who repented were baptized in the river Jordan. So many heard his message and were baptized that he became known as "John, the Baptizer."

Some who came from Jerusalem had been sent by the priests to find out if perhaps John was the Messiah, the great leader God was expected to send to be the Savior of the world.

"Who are you?" they asked John. "Are you the Messiah?"

"I am not!" he answered. "I am only a voice in the desert sent by God to declare that the day of His coming is near and to call upon all people to get ready! To tell you the truth, He is already here on the earth," he added, "but no one has recognized Him. When He is recognized, He will be seen to be far greater than I—so much greater that I will not be worthy to untie his shoes. I am baptizing with water, but He will baptize with the Holy Spirit."

The very next day, John saw Jesus coming toward him. Jesus was now a grown man, thirty years old, but He had not yet begun his ministry or announced who He was. He had been living quietly in Nazareth, working as a carpenter, perhaps helping to support His mother, Mary, and her younger children.

As Jesus drew nearer to John, John cried out, "Look! There is the Lamb of God! He has come to take away the sin of the world! This is the one I was talking about when I said, 'One far greater than I is coming.'"

As Jesus came on up to where John was standing, He said, "I have come to be baptized."

John was not prepared for that! He felt it should be the other way around, so he replied, "I need to be baptized by You, not You by me!"

"But I am asking you to do it," Jesus said. "It is important to fulfill all righteousness."

So, side by side, they walked down to the bank of the river Jordan, and there Jesus was baptized. Immediately afterward, as He was praying and looking up toward the sky, the Holy Spirit came down in the form of a dove and rested upon Him. Also, He heard a voice from Heaven, God's voice, saying, "You are my Son. I dearly love You and am well-pleased with what You have done." This was God's way of telling the people that Jesus was God's Messiah, the world's Savior. God had approved of the way Jesus had begun His ministry.

Prayer:

Dear God,
I want to follow Your plan for my life, too,
And honor You in all I say and do.
I want to do only what is right,
To walk always in Your light
Serving You with all my might.

I want to be the best that I can be, too,
For truth, for goodness, and for You,
So be my guide, both night and day,
And keep me in Your true and holy way.
Amen.

Questions for Discussion

1. Why was John called "The Baptizer?"
2. Describe John's appearance and the food that he ate.
3. What was John's message when he preached?
4. What did Jesus ask John to do and what was John's reply?
5. Describe what happened just after Jesus was baptized,
6. What did the voice from Heaven say?

CHAPTER TWELVE

PEER PRESSURE

What is peer pressure? It's the pressure your friends sometimes put on you to do something you know you should not do. Things like smoking a cigarette or taking a drink or experimenting with drugs. If you are afraid of being called "chicken," if you follow the *crowd* instead of your *conscience*, if you put what is "popular" ahead of what is "right," if "standing *in*" with your friends is more important than "standing *up*" for what you believe—if any or all of these things are problems for you, then you have a "peer pressure" problem.

This Bible story is about a man who had such a problem and how he struggled with it.

* * * * * * *

Nicodemus had heard a great deal about Jesus. So he made up his mind to go to see Jesus when He was in Jerusalem. Nicodemus was a Pharisee, and his closest friends were Pharisees too. The Pharisees were a religious group who, in the time of Jesus, had a great deal of influence with the Jewish people. They were very strict in their interpretation of the Ten Commandments and other Old Testament laws, and they openly criticized Jesus for doing such things as healing on the Sabbath. Some even threatened to kill Jesus if He came to Jerusalem. Nicodemus knew he would be criticized for going to see

Jesus. That explains why he decided to go at night. He wanted to keep his visit a secret.

Once he had arrived at the house where Jesus was staying and had been welcomed by Jesus, Nicodemus said, "Teacher, we have heard here in Jerusalem about Your mighty miracles in Galilee and know God must be with You. I have come to learn more about what You believe and teach."

Jesus's answer was not at all what Nicodemus expected. "Nicodemus," He said, "unless you are born again, you cannot enter the kingdom of Heaven."

No wonder Nicodemus was startled! Not only were the Pharisees the religious leaders of their day; they were very proud and quite satisfied with themselves. Jesus was reminding Nicodemus that, regardless of his good opinion about himself and regardless of his good reputation in Jerusalem, he needed to become a new and entirely different person.

Nicodemus seemed not to understand, so Jesus went on to explain:

"Nicodemus," He said, "do you remember that story in the book of Exodus about some of the people of Israel being bitten by snakes out in the wilderness? Moses was told by God to make a bronze snake and attach it to a pole. Those who looked up to the bronze snake in faith were saved. Well, one of

these days," he continued, "I will be lifted up so that everyone who believes in me may be saved." Then speaking very earnestly and looking straight into Nicodemus' eyes, Jesus added, "For God loved the world so much that He gave His only Son that everyone who believes in Him may have eternal life. Nicodemus, God sent me into the world, not to be the world's judge, but to be the world's Savior!"

Then and there Jesus was opening the door to the kingdom of Heaven for Nicodemus, offering to be his Savior and inviting him to become one of His followers. Why didn't he do it? Was it because of peer pressure? Because he knew what his friends, the Pharisees, would say? How sad that he passed up his great opportunity to become a follower of Jesus. So the night was still dark, very dark, in more ways than one, as he made his way back to his home.

In the days that followed, Nicodemus kept thinking about his visit with Jesus, but he couldn't find the courage to say anything to his friends about it. However, one day some weeks later, several of the Pharisees were discussing Jesus in Nicodemus' presence when one of them said with a sneer, "Is there a single one of us who believes that He is the Messiah? The stupid crowds from Galilee may think He is, but what do they know? We Pharisees know better!"

That was too much for Nicodemus! Remembering how kind Jesus had been to him and recalling His claim that He was the world's Savior, Nicodemus broke in, "Is it fair to condemn a man before he has had a chance to speak for himself?"

Then one of the Pharisees let him have it. "Are you one of the stupid Galileans too?" he sneered. "Read what is written in the Scriptures! No prophet ever came from Galilee!"

And Nicodemus drew back into his shell. The peer pressure was on, and he didn't have the courage to buck it!

There was one other Pharisee in Jerusalem who, like Nicodemus, admired Jesus very much, and who, also like Nicodemus and for the same reason, kept quiet about it. His name was Joseph, and in the Gospel of John, he is described as "a secret disciple of Jesus because of his fear of the Jewish leaders."

Just when he and Nicodemus became close friends or when they shared with each other their personal interest in Jesus, we do not know, but we do know that on the day Jesus was crucified they decided they would be *secret* disciples no longer! It is possible they were standing side by side near the cross as Jesus died and then and there decided what each would do.

So away they hurried—Joseph to secure permission from Pilate to take the body of Jesus down from the cross and bury it—Nicodemus to purchase white linen sheets in which to wrap it and fragrant ointment and spices with which to embalm it.

When they returned to Calvary and were standing at the foot of the cross, Nicodemus may have said, "Joseph, now I understand what He meant when He said to me, 'I will be lifted up from the earth that everyone who believes in me may be saved.'"

Then they loosened the nails, tenderly lifted the body of Jesus from the cross, and lowered it to the ground. There they wrapped it in layer after layer of linen, made fragrant with the abundance of the ointment and spices Nicodemus had brought. All the while they were hearing jeers of ridicule and scorn from the crowd still milling around the hill. But they did not mind. What they were doing amounted to a public vote against the decision of the Jewish rulers to condemn Jesus. They were doing what even His disciples, now in hiding, had not dared to do. No longer did they care what the Jewish leaders might say. Peer pressure did not matter anymore! They wanted all the world to know they were *for* Jesus, that they believed in Him, loved Him, and intended to be His faithful disciples as long as they lived. Nicodemus and Joseph were ready to die for Him, if need be!

As they later walked homeward in the gathering darkness, having laid His body to rest in the rock-hewn tomb Joseph had provided, it was probably not of their final courageous deed that they were thinking, but of what cowards they had been earlier! They had done what they could, but there was so much more they might have done for Him and for His cause had they not waited until the last dark hour to declare their faith. It was so little and so late, when He had given so much!

Prayer: Dear God, make me brave whenever I am tempted to do something that I know Jesus would not want me to do.
I want to live always for the right.
I want to stand always against the wrong.
I want to serve You with all my might.
So, dear God, make and keep me strong.
Amen.

Questions for Discussion

1. Explain what "peer presure" is and give examples fom your own experience.
2. Who were the Pharisees and what were they like?
3. Why did Nicodemus want to visit Jesus? Why did he go at night?
4. What did Jesus invite Nicodemus to do, and why did he not accept the invitation?
5. In what way were Nicodemus and his friend Joseph alike?
6. Tell about the burial of Jesus and what each of the two friends did.
7. Why did their deed call for courage?

CHAPTER THIRTEEN

THE COWARD WHO BECAME A HERO

Do you know what a "lapidary" is? Well, the diamond, as you know, is a very beautiful and a very valuable precious stone. Most likely it is the jewel in the ring your father gave to your mother when they became engaged to be married several years ago.

But quite a few things were done with that diamond before it was mounted in your mother's ring. Its "life" began, we might say as a "diamond in the rough." First, someone had to find it—and someone did, perhaps in a dark mine down below the surface of the earth in South Africa. Then, having been found, it had to be separated from the sand and dirt, and finally put into the hands of a lapidary.

And what is a lapidary? A lapidary is a skillful jeweler who can do amazing things with diamonds and other precious stones. In the case of an uncut diamond, he first studies it carefully with two aims in mind. First, he wants to obtain the largest and most perfect stone or stones possible. Second, he wants to remove every flaw or defect.

The largest diamond ever discovered is known as the Cullinan diamond of South Africa. It was three times larger than any other diamond that has ever been discovered and weighed almost a pound and a half in its natural state.

A lapidary who knew what he was doing took that diamond into his shop, cleaned and polished it, and divided it into nine beautiful stones—not all of the same size, of course, but each a very handsome and a very valuable gem. Two of those gems are worn in the crowns of the King and Queen of England. You see, a lapidary can do amazing things with diamonds and other precious stones!

* * * * * * *

The diamond reminds us of what Jesus did with the men He called to be His disciples. Most certainly they were "diamonds in the rough" at the beginning. During the three years Jesus and His disciples were together, they were not only learning from Him, but they were being changed for the better.

Take the one whose name was Simon Peter, for example.

One day—this was near the end of Jesus' ministry—being with His disciples in a quiet place, Jesus asked them, "Who do the people think I am?"

"Some think one thing and some another," they replied. "Some say You are John the Baptist, whom King Herod beheaded, risen from the dead. Some say you are one of the prophets or Elijah sent by God to prepare the way for the coming of the Christ."

Jesus was leading up to the all-important question. After a pause He said, "But what about you? Who do you say I am?"

It was Simon Peter who broke in with the positive answer: "Master, You are the Christ, the Son of the living God."

Jesus was deeply moved, not only by what Peter had said, but by the forceful way in which he said it.

"It was my Father in Heaven who revealed this truth to you!" He said in reply, "and bless you for saying it!" Then He added, "Your name has been 'Simon,' but from now on it will be 'Peter.' I will build my church, and not even the gates of Hell will be able to stand against it!"

A few days later Jesus was trying to explain to His disciples that since He was the Christ, as Peter had said, He would have to go to Jerusalem and suffer and die in order to become the world's Savior. His words came as a shock to all of them! Up to this time they had expected Him to become their king and wear a crown, not die on a cross!

Again it was Peter who spoke out.

"Oh, no!" he exclaimed. "That should never happen to You!"

Jesus' reply to Peter was a stern rebuke, and this time He called him a name very different from "Peter."

"Get away from me, Satan! You are a stumbling block to me. You are more interested in what you would have me do than what my Father in Heaven would have me do!"

That time Peter was a problem to Jesus, not an inspiration!

There was another time when Peter was a problem to Jesus. It was on the last night before Jesus' crucifixion. Jesus had spent the evening with His disciples in the home of a friend where they had had the first Communion service together. Now they were on their way to the Garden of Gethsemane where Jesus was going to pray. At the gate of the garden they stopped, and turning to His disciples, Jesus said with great sadness in His voice, "Tonight all of you will desert me, like sheep running in all directions when their shepherd is killed!"

Again Peter broke in, "Not I!" he exclaimed. "No matter what these others may do, I will never desert you!"

But Jesus, knowing what Peter would do, replied, "Listen, Peter, as I tell you the truth! This very night, before the rooster crows in the morning to announce the dawn, you will deny me three times."

"No, never!" Peter exclaimed, "Even if I have to die with You, I will never deny You!"

And, of course, he meant it. It was the hero in his soul that was speaking. But there was a coward in his soul too. Like all of us, Peter was a "two-in-one" person, and later that night "the coward" took command.

After having been arrested, Jesus was in the house of the high priest where He was standing trial before the Jewish leaders. Peter had followed behind at a safe distance and was sitting around a fire in the yard with the soldiers who had arrested Jesus, trying to keep warm and hoping he wouldn't be recognized.

But someone came by and looking at him said, "This man was with Jesus."

That moment was Peter's big opportunity to stand up for Jesus, to say, "Yes, I was and that is why I am here. I know He is innocent and should be set free. He should never have been arrested!" But instead Peter said, "No, I don't even know Him." A little later, another person

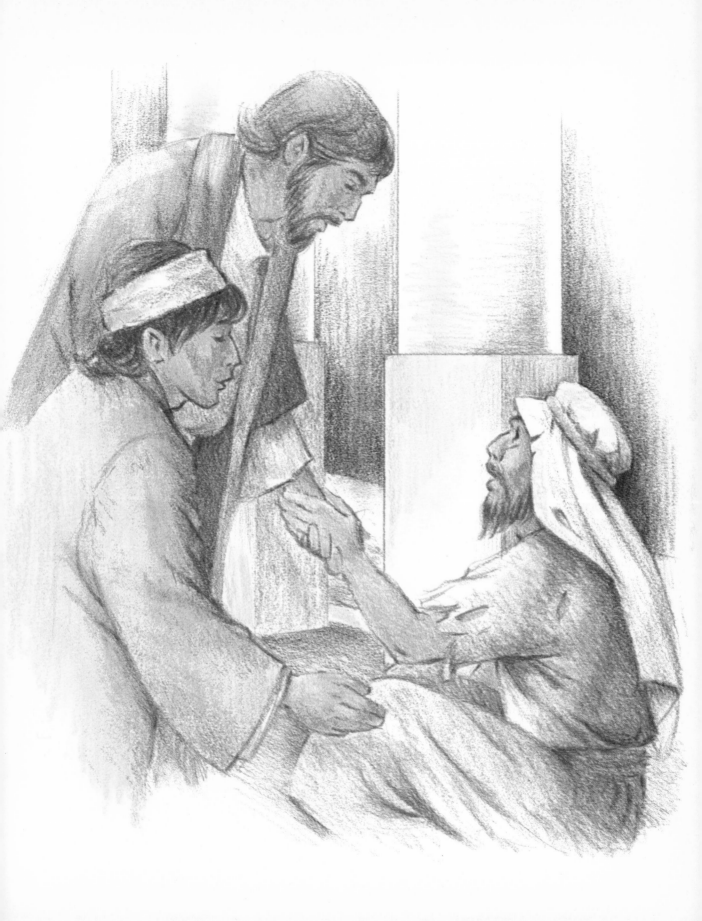

came by and said, "I know this man was with Jesus!" But again Peter denied that he even knew Him.

About an hour later, someone standing around the fire looked him straight in the face and said, "You must be one of His followers. From the way you talk anybody can tell you are from Galilee and that's where He is from."

By now Peter was really in a tight corner! And he exploded, "I don't even know the fellow, I tell you! I don't know what you're talking about!"

Just at that point, not far away, a rooster crowed! And in a flash it all came back—the words of warning Jesus had spoken just a few hours before! Ashamed beyond words, Peter got up and started to leave. On the way out, he looked up toward the room where Jesus was being questioned by the Jewish leaders, and Jesus was looking straight at him. That look melted his heart, and he went out, leaned against a tree, and cried and cried!

Peter must have prayed, asking over and over to be forgiven for being such a coward and wondering if ever he would become the man Jesus had in mind when He said, "Your name will be Peter," which means a rock.

The happy ending to this story is that in time Peter did become just that, a rock! In the book of Acts he is the leader of the disciples going from place to place preaching, teaching, and healing as Jesus had done. More than once we read of how courageous he was! One example is in chapter 4, verse 13 of Acts where it is said: "When the Council (and this was the same Council that had tried and condemned Jesus to death!) saw how bold Peter and John were, they were amazed and realized this was because of what being with Jesus had done for them."

Thus the disciple, who was often a problem to Jesus, in time had become, as Jesus had predicted, Peter, the Rock! Or, to put it another way, a "diamond in the rough" had been transformed by a skillful and patient lapidary into a sparkling jewel!

Prayer: Lord Jesus, I don't want to ever be a coward.
I want to meet every test,
By doing my very best;
I want to obey always, and never delay;
I want to become brave, strong, and true;
So be patient with me day after day,
And help me to become more and more like You.
Amen.

Questions for Discussion

1. When Jesus asked His disciples "Who do people think I am?" what was their answer?
2. What was His next question? What was Peter's answer?
3. What did Peter say when Jesus predicted that His disciples were going to desert Him?
4. What was Jesus' answer?
5. Describe what happened to Peter when he was sitting around the fire trying to keep warm?
6. Why did he leave? Where did he go? What did he do?
7. What evidence do we find in the book of Acts that he later became a different man?

CHAPTER FOURTEEN

FROM HOTHEAD TO LOVING HEART

B'jorn Borg from Sweden was one of the world's greatest tennis players. As I watched him play, I was amazed at his calmness under pressure. He was never upset when he missed a shot, and he never questioned the call of a linesman or the umpire!

But he was not always like that. As a little boy learning to play the game, he had an ugly temper. Sometimes when he missed a shot or served a double fault, he would slam the ball against the fence or throw his racquet down, with angry words pouring out.

His mother, who very much wanted B'jorn to become a good player, would take his racquet away from him, sometimes for a week at a time, and give him a little lecture. "B'jorn," she would say, "until you first learn to control yourself, you will never be able to control your racquet!" In time he learned that lesson and became a true champion.

This Bible story is about a man who, like B'jorn Borg, had a hard time learning how to control his temper. But fortunately, he had a very wonderful Teacher.

* * * * * * *

Had we known what he was like when Jesus called him to be one of His twelve disciples, we might have wondered why Jesus ever chose him. Or having chosen him, why He did not send him back home and choose someone else. His name was John, and at the beginning of his relationship with Jesus, he apparently had a violent temper.

So also did his brother James. It was so evident that Jesus gave them a very appropriate nickname, "Sons of Thunder" or "Hotheads." (See Mark 3:17.)

There were times when Jesus had to be very direct and firm. For example, there was a time when John saw a man trying to drive an evil spirit out of an afflicted man by using the name of Jesus. Rushing up to the man, he shouted, "Who are you to use the name of Jesus in trying to work a miracle? You have no right to use His name when you are not one of His disciples!"

John was still boiling when he reported to Jesus what had happened. "Master," he said, "I did my best to get him to stop because he wasn't one of Your followers."

John waited, expecting Jesus to commend him for what he had tried to do. But instead, he heard Jesus say, "Don't you see that if the man was trying to heal in my name, he is on our side? Whoever is not against us is for us. Anyone who gives you a cup of water in my name will certainly not lose his reward."

There was another day when John (and his brother James, too) needed and received a still more severe rebuke. Jesus and His disciples were passing through Samaria on their way to Jerusalem to observe the Passover. They needed lodging for the night, so Jesus sent John and James on ahead to make

arrangements in the next town. But they were turned down everywhere they asked.

When they returned and reported to Jesus how they had been turned away again and again, John said, "Master, let us call down fire from Heaven and burn them up!"

Jesus, of course, rebuked them. "When will you learn that God sent me into the world, not to kill people, but to save them?" He said. Then quickly Jesus led them to another town where they found lodging for the night.

Just how often Jesus had to remind or rebuke John about his temper we do not know, but we do know they were together as Teacher and disciple (and the word "disciple" means "pupil") for three years; and in time John learned not only to control his anger, but to replace it with love and gentleness. For proof of that, we go in imagination to Calvary. There, as we read in the Gospel which John himself later wrote, Jesus, as He was dying, looked down and saw His mother and John standing side by side at the foot of the cross.

With a heart full of love for His mother and full of trust in John, Jesus said, "John, my dear friend, take her and care for her as if she were your own mother."

And to Mary, "Mother, go and live with him as if he were your own son."

Then and there John took Mary into his care. He took her to his home and tended to her needs as lovingly and tenderly as if she had been his own mother.

It is not surprising that from then on John was known as "The Apostle of Love." In a letter he later wrote which is in our Bible, he said, "Dear friends, let us love one another, for love comes from God. Everyone who loves has been born of God and knows God. ... God is love. Whoever lives in love lives in God, and God in him. No one has ever seen God; but if we love each other, God lives in us and his love is made complete in us" (1 John 4:7, 16, 12 *New International Version*).

So, to sum up our story, a man who was a "son of thunder" or a hothead when he first met Jesus, in time became "the apostle of love." The explanation in one sentence: In Jesus, John had a warm friend and a wonderful teacher; and in John, Jesus had an attentive and obedient pupil!

Prayer: Lord Jesus, I don't want to be a hothead. So please be my Teacher and my Friend, as well as my Savior. Do help me to control my temper and to become a gentle, loving person like Your disciple John. Amen.

Questions for Discussion

1. What nickname did Jesus give John and his brother James, and what did the name mean? Why was it appropriate?
2. Why did John try to stop the man who was trying to heal another man?
3. What did Jesus say when John told Him about it?
4. Why were the Samaritans unwilling to give Jesus and His disciples lodging for the night?
5. What did John suggest should be done and what was Jesus' reply?
6. What did Jesus, speaking to John from the cross, ask him to do?
7. By what title was he known from that time on?

CHAPTER FIFTEEN

TWO BUILDERS

It is called the "Sermon on the Mount" because Jesus preached it as He sat on the side of a mountain. A great crowd was present and they were good listeners—that is, if good listening meant simply being quiet and paying attention to what was being said.

Also the people liked what they heard. Perhaps during the sermon again and again they whispered in their hearts—possibly some of them said it aloud:

"Amen, Amen!"

"What a preacher!"

"That's the kind of preaching the world needs and the kind we want to hear!"

Perhaps after the sermon the people kept on talking about it and about what a fine preacher Jesus was. "He really knows what He is talking about," they said, "and He says it like He means it. He is so different from the teachers we hear in our synagogues week after week!"

Jesus knew how well his sermon was being received. Even as He was speaking, He must have been encouraged by the eager attention of the people to what He was saying—but He was also concerned!

Because, you see, He was preaching not to *please* people, but to *change* them. It was not *applause* He was seeking, but *action.* It was not how people *felt* that mattered to Him, but what they *did!*

So, as He came to the end of His sermon, He asked a sharp question, "Why do you call me 'Lord, Lord,' and do not do what I say?"

Then to drive home the point that "actions speak louder than words," He told them a story.

* * * * * * *

Had He been telling the story today, it would probably have gone something like this:

Once upon a time there were two men who decided to build, each for himself and his family, a summer home. Also, each chose and bought a lot near the seashore where there would be cooling breezes from the ocean by day and night and opportunities for swimming and fishing. Let us call the two men Mr. A and Mr. B.

Mr. A was the first to start building. The highest part of his lot was a sand dune. He hired workmen to level it off, then brought in cement and mortar and laid a concrete foundation before he began the actual building.

Mr. B came by and saw what Mr. A was doing and asked about the cost of the concrete foundation. When he found it was quite expensive, he said to himself, "I can save that expense. There's a sand dune on my lot, too, and it is well back from the beach. I will level it off, wet the sand and pack it down, then

bring in lumber and build my house on it. And so he did.

When the two houses were completed, both looked very beautiful from the outside. In fact, from the outside they looked very much alike! Both families were very happy as they moved in. They received many compliments from neighbors and friends about their respective houses.

Both houses were also attractively furnished inside. As a matter of fact, the only real difference between the two was that Mr. A's house had a concrete foundation, while Mr. B's had been built on the sand. That did not seem to matter in the spring and early summer when there was lots of sunshine and only an occasional thundershower in the afternoon.

But during the late summer and early fall, the heavier rainstorms began to come and some of the sand began to wash away from the dune on which Mr. B had built his house.

One day severe weather was forecast, so Mr. A and Mr. B packed up their families and moved inland to where it was safer.

Once it was safe to return to the beach, both families headed back to see what damage, if any, had been done to their homes.

Mr. A arrived first. The yard was littered with leaves and broken limbs, and one tree had blown down, but his house was still standing with no noticeable damage. Also the furniture inside was still dry and safe.

But in the case of Mr. B's home, it was no longer a house at all, but a tangled mass of lumber at the foot of the sand dune, with the furniture soaked and broken. The house was completely demolished.

From this story we learn that, if we are truly wise, we will build our lives upon the solid foundation of Jesus' teachings. And that means not only that we will listen to His Words, but that we will obey them. To listen and not obey is to be as foolish as the man who built his house upon the sand!

Prayer:

Lord Jesus,
Make me wise to listen
To everything You say,
And not only to listen,
But to obey;
To do it day after day,
So my faith may be strong
No matter what comes along,
Like a house that stands every shock
Because it is built upon a rock.
Amen.

Questions for Discussion

1. In Jesus' story about the two builders, describe how Mr. A began building his house.
2. How did Mr. B begin?
3. When completed, how did the two houses look from the outside?
4. What did the storm do to the house of Mr. A?
5. What did it do to the house of Mr. B?
6. What explains the difference?
7. What do we learn from this story?

CHAPTER SIXTEEN

ARE YOU A GOOD LISTENER?

Just how popular or unpopular would you say Jesus was as a teacher when He was on the earth?

The correct answer is, with people in general, He was very popular. Great crowds followed Him and listened to His teaching.

But many of the Jewish leaders were against Him. They were jealous of His popularity and influence, and one day when He was teaching in the courtyard of the temple, they ordered the temple guards to go and arrest Him.

But the temple guards became so interested in what He was saying that they came back without Him, giving as their excuse, "We never before heard anyone teach as He does!" (See John 7:32, 45, 46.)

Although Jesus was very popular as a teacher, He as by no means satisfied with the way people listened! He knew that what He said was not reaching their hearts and changing their lives. One day He expressed His deep concern about this situation by telling the following story.

* * * * * * *

Once upon a time there was a farmer who went out to sow his seed.

The farmer, Jesus later explained to His disciples, represented himself teaching the people, while the farmer's seeds represented the words He spoke as He taught.

The field where the farmer sowed his seed represented the hearts of the people who heard Jesus' words. Now in the field there were *four kinds of soil.* So, according to Jesus, there were four kinds of people who listened to His words.

First, in the case of the farmer, there was a path which ran through his field. Some of the seeds he sowed fell on the path where the soil was hard, and the birds flew in and gobbled them up.

Just so, according to Jesus, the hearts of some of the people who heard Him were so hard that His words never got below the surface, or as a familiar expression of ours puts it, "They went in one ear and out the other!"

On the edge of the farmer's field was a second kind of soil which might be called thin or shallow—only an inch or two of soil and underneath a ledge of rock. The seeds that fell on that soil sprouted, but after a few days, when their roots reached the rock, the plants withered under the heat of the sun and died.

Just so, according to Jesus, among His hearers were some who at first were enthusiastic about His teaching. Perhaps they said to themselves, if not out loud, "Amen! Hallelujah!"

But their enthusiasm did not last! As soon as they ran into persecution or ridicule, they gave up and became "dropouts!"

On another edge of the farmer's field was a briar patch, and some of his seed

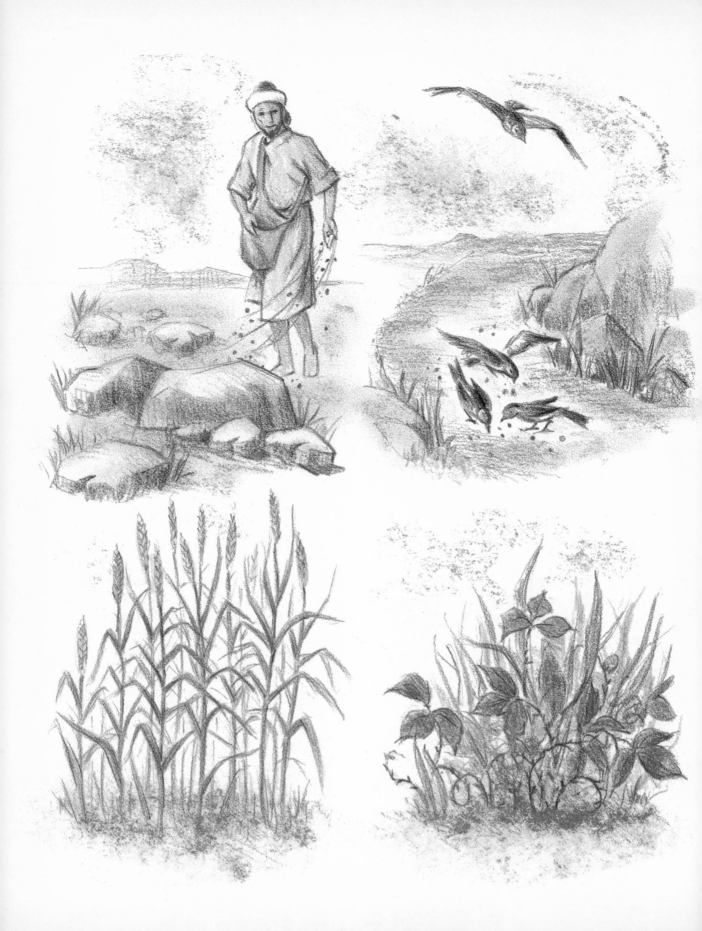

fell there. Those seeds sprouted, too, but the briars grew faster than the plants of grain, used up the nourishment in the soil, and crowded the plants out.

Again, according to Jesus, among those who listened to His teaching were some whose hearts were so full of worry or whose minds were so occupied with thoughts about money and how to make more, that the words He spoke never had a chance to take root and grow.

But, and this is the bright part of the story, there were other parts of the farmer's field that had been plowed and were soft and fertile. "Good soil," Jesus called it.

The farmer's seeds that fell into that soil not only sprouted and sprang up, but continued to grow until in time they produced an abundant harvest—sometimes a hundred times more than the seeds that were sown!

When Jesus referred to good soil, He had in mind "good hearers"—those who listen to His words not only with their ears, but also with their minds and hearts! They were people who paid attention to what He said until they understood it, then applied it to their lives!

One thing more to remember about this story is this: God in His wisdom and love has preserved Jesus' teachings in His holy book, the Bible. He knew that we would need to hear the lessons Jesus taught many years ago.

Jesus not only was, but still is, the greatest and wisest of all teachers. He still speaks to us and tells us how He wants us to live and what He wants us to become. *How?*

Sometimes as we hear His words in a sermon.

Sometimes as we read in our New Testament the very words He spoke when He was on the earth.

Sometimes as we listen to a good Sunday-school teacher or to a loving father or mother explain a verse or passage in the Bible.

Sometimes as we listen to His quiet voice speaking in our consciences.

So, whenever, wherever, or however He may speak to us today, let us be ready to give the same answer that the young Samuel did when, one night he heard his name called after he had gone to bed, and he answered, "Speak, Lord! For I am your servant, and I am listening!" (1 Samuel 3:10).

Prayer:

Dear God,
To me You have given
Ears to hear,
A mind to understand,
And a will to obey Your truth.
So, teach me day by day
That there's no other way
To be pleasing to Jesus
But to really listen, and to obey!
Amen.

Questions for Discussion

1. In the story Jesus told, name the four kinds of soil in the farmer's field.
2. What did each kind of soil represent when applied to the way people listened to Jesus' teaching?
3. Describe what happened to the seeds that fell in the good soil.
4. In what ways does Jesus speak to us today?
5. Discuss what it means for us to be really good listeners.

CHAPTER SEVENTEEN

TWO PRAYERS

It must have been a wonderful experience for the disciples of Jesus to hear Him pray. As a matter of fact, we know it was because in the Gospel of Luke we are told that one day, as Jesus was praying in a certain place, when He finished, one of His disciples said to Him, "Lord, teach us to pray" (Luke 11:1).

In answer to that request, Jesus gave to His disciples—and through them to us—what is known all over the world as "The Lord's Prayer," which, as you know, begins, "Our Father who art in Heaven." It is what might be called a model prayer. It is not just a prayer to be "repeated" in church or in a prayer meeting, but a prayer to guide us as to how and for what we should pray when we talk to God, using our own words.

More important than the words we use is our spirit or attitude when we pray— that is, how we feel toward God, toward ourselves, and toward others.

To teach that lesson, Jesus once told a story about two men who one day went up to the temple to pray. Their prayers were not at all alike. One was a very "good" prayer, and God was pleased with it and answered it.

The other was anything but a "good" prayer, and God did not answer it. Because, as we shall see, the man was really talking *about* himself and *to* himself rather than to God!

* * * * * * *

The story Jesus told went something like this:

As the Pharisee made his way toward the temple, he felt quite good about himself. He was looked up to because of his knowledge of the Bible and was often asked about the meaning of some of the difficult passages. He liked that and felt he really deserved it!

He was regular in attending the temple services and more than ready to give his advice. He wondered how many would be present for worship on this particular Sabbath morning and hoped they would notice the new bright cloak he was wearing. Once inside the temple, he remembered it was a "house of prayer," and that he himself should say one. But he had everything he needed, so what was there to ask for? And he couldn't think of anything that he had done that was wrong, so there was no need for confession.

Then he thought about thanksgiving. Yes, he had many things for which to be grateful.

Now, in our prayers of gratitude, we thank God for the beautiful world in which we live, for family and friends, for food and clothing, for God's love expressed in so many ways.

But in his prayer, the Pharisee mentioned none of these things. His prayer began and ended with himself. It was completely self-centered and went

something like this: "God, I thank you that I am not like other people such as robbers, murderers, and cheaters."

At that point, he looked around and saw a tax collector standing in a corner at the back of the temple. In the time of Jesus, tax collectors were called "publicans" and were despised by the Jews, not only because they collected taxes for the hated Romans, but because they often charged more than was due and kept it for themselves.

Seeing this tax collector in the temple, the Pharisee added another sentence to his prayer: "I am especially thankful that I am not like that tax collector. As you know, Lord, I am an honest man. Twice a week I do without dinner and give the money to the poor. I give one-tenth of my income to the support of the temple and am present for worship every Sabbath day. I do thank You, God, for how good I am." Such was the prayer the Pharisee prayed. You see, he really wasn't praying at all—he was only patting himself on the back!

In the back corner of the temple the tax collector was praying too. Coming into God's house had made him think about God's holiness and goodness and of how unworthy he was. Deep within his heart he knew that he was a sinner, and that above everything else he needed to be forgiven. Also deep within his heart he felt that God was merciful and kind and would forgive him if he was truly sorry and asked to be forgiven.

So with his head bowed and with his hand on his heart he prayed, "Dear God, be merciful to me a sinner!"

It was a short and very simple prayer, but it was from his heart. God heard his prayer and answered it.

After that, his conscience no longer troubled him! He was at peace with God, at peace with the world, and at peace with himself.

After the temple service, the Pharisee walked home, too, but with no new blessing, because he had not felt he needed any!

Jesus told this story, the Bible says, for the benefit of those who boasted of their own goodness and looked down on everyone else. He was trying to teach them the same lesson Paul had in mind when he wrote to Christians in Rome and also in Philippi, "Do not be conceited or think too highly of yourself. Never act from selfishness or pride, but in humility count others better than yourselves" (Romans 12:3; Philippians 2:3).

Surely that is a lesson we, too, need to remember and to practice!

Prayer: Dear God, why should I ever be proud? Everything I have is mine only because of Your great goodness to me! That leaves much for which I should be grateful, but nothing of which I should boast. So may I keep on singing Your praises, but never my own! In Jesus' name, amen.

Questions for Discussion

1. Can you pray "The Lord's Prayer"? Why did Jesus teach it?
2. Describe the Pharisee who went up to the temple.
3. What did he say in his prayer?
4. What did the publican say in his prayer?
5. How did he know it was answered?
6. Why did the Pharisee receive no new blessing?
7. What lesson does this story teach?

CHAPTER EIGHTEEN

A GOOD NEIGHBOR

He was a "sharp" lawyer, but not as "sharp" as he thought he was! He thought he could outsmart Jesus in a discussion about religion, but he found out otherwise.

When the Bible calls him "a lawyer," it means he was an expert in his knowledge of the laws in the Old Testament. He might be compared in our day to a professor in a Bible college.

From his point of view, Jesus was a young rabbi from Galilee who needed to be examined and "kept in his place"!

So the lawyer began with a question, and he was polite in the way he asked it, "Teacher, what must I do to have eternal life?"

Jesus handed the question back. "You are an expert in the law," He said. "What does your Bible say?"

And here the lawyer showed that he was truly a keen student of the Old Testament. He picked out one verse from the book of Deuteronomy and another from the book of Leviticus, put the two together and came up with, "It says, 'Love the Lord your God with all your heart and with all your soul and with all your strength and with all your mind' and 'Love your neighbor as yourself'" (Deuteronomy 6:5 and Leviticus 19:18).

Jesus knew that the lawyer had given a great answer and so he said, "Right! Obey these two commandments and you will have eternal life."

The lawyer had not expected that! He had come to *argue* with Jesus, not to be preached to! Jesus was getting entirely too personal. To get back on the discussion track, he said, "But who is my neighbor?"

Now, as you may know, the word "neighbor" means simply, "someone who lives nearby." But to the Jews in Old Testament times and also in the time of Jesus, a neighbor was not just *anyone* who lived nearby. A person from another nation or race, called a foreigner, was not considered a neighbor even though he lived on the same street.

The answer the lawyer was about to hear from Jesus was very different from that! It came in the form of a story in which Jesus would teach, "Your neighbor is anyone who needs your help."

* * * * * * *

The story Jesus told went something like this:

One day there was a Jewish man who was making a trip from Jerusalem to Jericho, a distance of about twenty miles. The road from Jerusalem to Jericho was a dangerous road to travel even in the daytime. It was known as "Robbers' Road." It was a downhill road, winding its way through a narrow gorge with rocky hills on both sides, and there was no police protection of any kind. As the Jewish man made his way down this road, two robbers armed with clubs jumped out from behind a cliff, stopped him, and demanded his money. They beat him over the head with their clubs, took everything he had including his clothes, and left him unconscious beside the road.

A priest came up the road and saw him lying over in the ditch.

"My, my!" he said to himself. "I do believe the man has been beaten. I suppose I should go over and see."

But just then he remembered that he would have to hurry to keep from being late for the worship service in the temple.

"Surely someone else will be by soon and will help the poor man," he said to himself and rode on.

A little later, another man came along the road. He too was quite religious—he was a Levite, which means he was in training to become a priest and often helped in the services of the temple.

When the Levite saw the man in the ditch, he walked over to get a better look at him, and said, "How terrible! The crime situation is getting worse and worse! It is a shame that the Romans don't provide a police patrol for this road. Those robbers could be back any moment; they could rob me and beat me up too. I had better hurry on."

The poor man in the ditch was growing weaker all the while and would probably have died. But, fortunately for him, a third man came by. He was a Samaritan by race. To the Jews, Samaritans were a mixed race called "half-breeds," and for this reason most Jews looked down on them and had nothing to do with them.

This Samaritan knew that, but it did not matter to him that the man in the ditch was Jewish. Nor did it matter to him that the bandits might return any moment. His heart went out to the wounded man. Quickly he opened the bag of provisions he had with him, knelt down beside the man, gave him a drink to revive him, soothed the bruised places on his body with oil, and bandaged his wounds.

Then he lifted him up on his donkey, and with his arm around him, walked beside him until they came to an inn several miles down the road.

There the Samaritan tied his donkey to the hitching post in the yard, then helped the wounded man inside and onto a couch where he could lie down. To the innkeeper he said, "I found this man unconscious beside the road. I want a room large enough for both of us with two beds so we can spend the night. Also, send us up some food. I will take care of him through the night and hopefully he will be better by morning."

Then he paid the bill and, with the hurt man leaning on his arm, followed the innkeeper to the room assigned to them. Before their supper arrived, he poured water into the basin in the room, washed the man's face and hands, bathed his feet, and redressed his wounds.

The next morning the man was much better, but still not able to travel on his own. So, as the Samaritan checked out, he said to the innkeeper, "I have an important engagement and can delay no longer. My friend is still not able to travel. So here is money to provide for another night's lodging and food. Let him stay longer if he needs to and take care of him. On my way back in a few days I will stop by and pay for any additional ex-

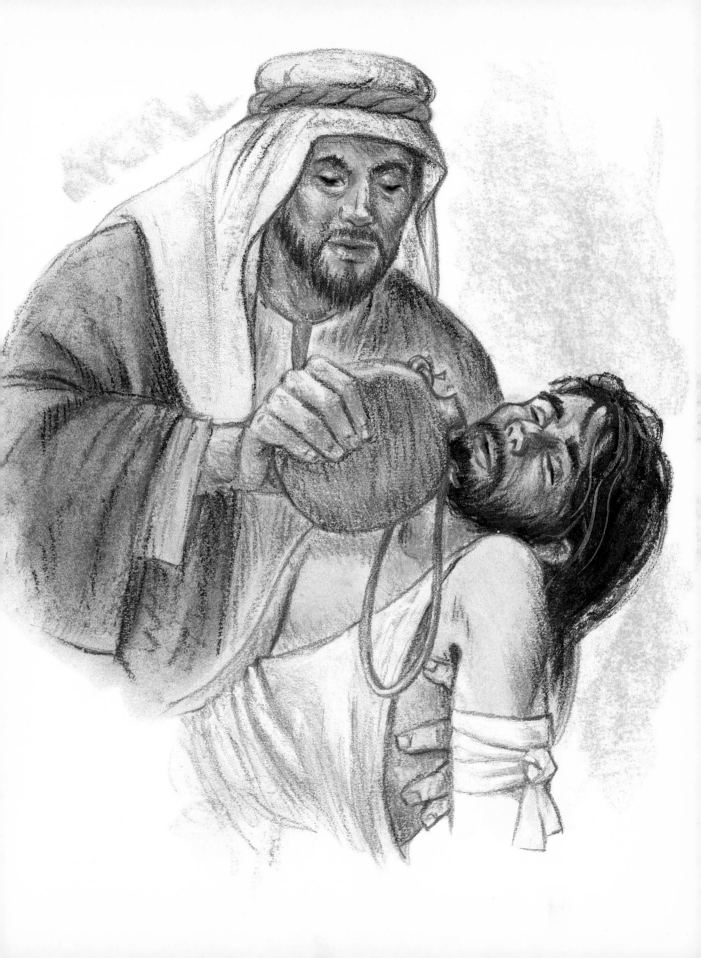

pense you may have."

Such was the story Jesus told the lawyer in answer to his question, "Who is my neighbor?" But Jesus did not end it there. He asked the lawyer another question, "Which one of the three men was a neighbor to the hurt man?"

The lawyer knew he should say, "The Samaritan." But being a Jew, he couldn't bring himself to recognize a Samaritan as the "hero" in the story. So instead he said, "The one who was kind to him." And still that was not the end of the story. Perhaps the lawyer wanted it to be. Already he was feeling far from comfortable—having to listen to a story in which Jesus had made a Samaritan "the hero" and two of the lawyers' fellow Jews, a priest and a Levite, the "villains." The Rabbi from Galilee was proving to be much sharper than he had expected. He was more than ready for the discussion to end. But, as he turned to leave, Jesus added, "Now that you know what a neighbor is, go and be one!"

And those words, I'm sure you will agree, were meant for us as well as for the lawyer!

Questions for Discussion

1. In Jesus' story, what did the priest do when he saw the wounded man in the ditch?
2. What did the Levite do?
3. What did the Samaritan do?
4. The Samaritan might be called "a sharing person." Name four things he "shared" with the wounded man.
5. Why do you think the Samaritan stopped to help when the other men did not? Think of a situation in which you can be a "good Samaritan."

CHAPTER NINETEEN

WISE OR FOOLISH PREPARATION?

Is it possible to be a Christian and still be happy? Most certainly Jesus meant for the answer to this question to be, "Yes!"

Once He said to His disciples, "These things I have spoken to you that my joy might be in you and that your joy might be full."

Also, in His great Sermon on the Mount, He said, "Rejoice and be glad, for great is your reward in Heaven. At the beginning of that sermon He used the word "blessed" or "happy" nine times. Also, again and again in His teaching He compared His kingdom to a banquet or a wedding . So if we are not happy in our faith, we are missing something Jesus meant for us to have! And to miss being in His kingdom would be to miss the highest joy of all!

* * * * * * *

To illustrate this, Jesus once told a story that went something like this:

Ten bridesmaids were as happy as could be! Also they were "all-a-flutter" getting ready for the wedding and the banquet.

In their country and in their time, the wedding ceremony was quite different from what it is our own country. In Palestine, which was their country, weddings usually took place at night and were followed by a banquet in the home of the bride. Also, it was the custom for the best friends of the groom and the bride to go out to meet the groom as he came from his home and to surround him with joyous singing and with laughter as he made his way to the home of his bride where the wedding and the banquet would take place. Each guest was expected to carry a lighted lamp as a token of welcome and which would light the path along which the wedding party was to pass.

It was to participate in such a procession that the ten bridesmaids were busy preparing—and except for one thing their preparation was the same.

They were all dressed alike, they had all received the same invitation, and all knew the place to which they were to go. Also, they all started out at the same time, and each carried a lighted lamp.

But five of them were carrying, in addition to a lighted lamp, a flask in which was an extra supply of oil.

In due time they all arrived at the place where they were to meet the bridegroom. They waited patiently for quite a while, but he was later than anyone expected. As a matter of fact, he did not arrive until midnight.

By that time, with their lamps burning all the while, all ten bridesmaids were dozing as they sat beside the road.

Then, all of a sudden someone shouted, "Wake up! The bridegroom is coming! It's time to go meet him!"

All ten bridesmaids were in a dither as

they noticed their lamps were flickering and about to go out because the oil in each was all but used up.

The five who had brought extra oil quickly refilled their lamps, trimmed their wicks, and were soon ready to meet the bridal procession.

The other five were in a panic! "Give us some of your oil," they pleaded, "our lamps are about to go out!"

"We are sorry, but we can't," the others answered. "We just brought enough to refill our own lamps."

Knowing it would be a disgrace to greet the bridegroom without a lighted lamp, the five who had no oil rushed away to buy some. But since it was midnight, all the shops were closed. Finally they found a shop whose owner lived in a room just above it. They shouted to him until he awakened and came to the window. He finally agreed to come down and sell them the oil they needed.

In the meantime, back at the bride's home, the wedding banquet was almost over. So when the five tardy bridesmaids finally arrived, they found the door locked and the porter would not let them in. They had lost out because their preparation had been "too little and too late!"

In telling this story, Jesus called the five bridesmaids who missed the banquet "foolish." The others He called, "wise." He was teaching His disciples, and through them teaching us, that the best things in life come, not to those who wait, but to those who are best prepared.

Prayer: Lord Jesus, help me always to be ready to do Your will and to be prepared for whatever may come. In Jesus' name, amen.

Questions for Discussion

1. In what ways were the ten "bridesmaids" all alike?
2. In what one way were they different?
3. What did the ten do while they waited for the bridegroom to arrive? And when did he arrive?
4. Why were five of them in a panic, and what did they do?
5. What did they find when they finally arrived at the wedding banquet?
6. Are you ready for Jesus' return? What do you need to do to be better prepared?

CHAPTER TWENTY

USING YOUR TALENTS

Did you ever wonder why some people have so many more talents or abilities than others?

Jesus once told a story which teaches that to God, the all-important question is not how many talents we have, but what we do with those we do have.

Had Jesus been telling the story today, it might have gone something like this:

Once there was a prosperous business man, president of his own company, who decided to extend his business to certain countries abroad. To open the new outlets he had in mind required him to make a trip overseas.

After all arrangements for his trip had been completed, he called in three of his trusted employees and offered to each a new challenge and opportunity.

To the first he said, "As you know, this trip abroad is for business purposes, and I do not know how long I will be gone. But while I am away, I would like for the money my company has to earn more. Here is a check for $10,000 made out to you personally. Invest it, using your best judgment, and see how much you can earn for me while I am gone."

"I will do my best," the first employee promised, and left with his $10,000 check.

Next came the second employee to whom the company president gave a check for $5,000. He, too, thanked his employer, promised to do his best, and left with his $5,000 check.

After him came the third employee to whom the company president gave a $2,000 check. This third man expressed no thanks to his employer, nor did he make any promise.

But a few days later, after his employer had left on his trip, the third employee said to himself, "Who does he think he is anyway? Expecting me to work harder while he is away!"

And with that he put his check in an envelope and tucked it into the bottom drawer of his desk.

In the meantime, the first employee who had received the $10,000 check found an acre lot just outside the city limits which he considered a good real estate investment. With his $10,000 he bought it. Sometime later a housing developer became interested in it and paid him $20,000 for it.

The second employee used his $5,000 as a down payment on the purchase of a downtown apartment. Shortly afterward he rented it as an office to a business friend, carefully saving the rent he received. He, too, in a short while doubled the amount he had invested.

Both of these employees felt it was an honor to have their boss entrust them with his money. They were happy for an opportunity to show their gratitude by making these investments for him. Also, they were overjoyed when they heard he had returned from his long trip and each was eager to make his report!

When the first was called in to the president's office, the two shook hands. Then the president asked, "Well, how did you do with the money I left you?"

"I am happy to report your company has continued to prosper in your absence," he said. "I had the good fortune to run into a real estate deal, so your $10,000 is now worth $20,000."

"Excellent!" the president replied. "You have proved yourself fully worthy of my trust. As your reward I am promoting you to the head of your department with a 50% increase in salary. Also I am hosting a special dinner tomorrow to cel-

ebrate my safe return. We will expect you and your wife as honored guests."

When the second employee came in, he reported, "Sir, I used the $5,000 you gave me to invest in an apartment which I was able to rent as an office. Your $5,000 is now worth $10,000."

"Excellent!" replied the president. "You have measured up fully to my expectations." Then the president added that the second employee also would be promoted to a new position with a 50% increase in salary. Also, he and his wife were invited to the special dinner on the following night.

When the third employee came in, he did not shake hands with his boss.

"Sir," he began as he held his $2,000 check in hand, "after working forty hours per week in your plant, I needed time to rest and to be with my family. I didn't think it was fair for you to expect me to work overtime. Besides, don't you have enough money without expecting us to work like slaves for you?

"I decided just to put the check you gave me in my desk drawer. Here it is, just like it was the day you gave it to me."

The president could hardly believe his ears! His other two employees had been so gracious and respectful, and this third one was charging him with being a slave driver! He held his rising anger in for a moment, then let go, "You lazy, evil-minded scoundrel! Why did you not refuse to take the $2,000 when I offered it to you? And since you did take it, you might at least have deposited it in the bank where it would have drawn a reasonable amount of interest! You have failed miserably to live up to what I expected of you! You are fired!" And the president ordered him out of his office!

Jesus gave His story a sad ending to teach the sad outcome that sooner or later comes to those who fail to make use of the talents God has given to them.

But in the case of the other two employees, we do have a happy ending because the story also points to the happy outcome for who make good use of their God-given talents. What really counts with God is not how many talents we have, but what we do with the talents we do have!

Prayer:

Dear God,
I may not have many talents, but I do have some,
And may I not let thinking about those I do not have
Keep me from using the talents I do have—
May I use them to make the world better and to glorify You.
Amen.

Questions for Discussion

1. What did the weatlhy businessman do before he went overseas and what were his instructions?
2. What did employee No. 1 do with his money?
3. What did employee No. 2 do with his money?
4. What did employee No. 3 do with his money?
5. What rewards did employees No. 1 and No. 2 receive?
6. What did No. 3 receive?
7. Name two or three talents you have.
8. What are you doing with them?

CHAPTER TWENTY-ONE

RUNAWAY SON COMES HOME

As we read about Jesus in the Bible, it seems to us that He was so kind and good that no one could have found in Him anything to criticize. But, as a matter of fact, the Jewish religious leaders of His day, called Scribes and Pharisees, were continually opposing and criticizing Him.

One day they said, "Look at those sinners and tax collectors listening to Him. We hear that sometimes He even sits down and eats with them. If He were really God's Son, He wouldn't keep company with such people!"

Jesus knew what they were saying. And He told a story to show that God loves everybody. He wants every sinner, no matter how bad he may be, to know he is loved and to come back to God.

* * * * * * *

If Jesus were telling the story today, it would probably go something like this:

He wasn't a bad boy—at least at this stage of his life, he wasn't. But he was fed up with home and the work on the farm. He wanted to be out on his own. He felt his father was too strict—always telling him what to do and what not to do. After all, he wasn't a child anymore, and he didn't like to be treated like one!

One day he decided to tell his father how he felt.

"Dad," he said, "it isn't that I don't appreciate all you've done for me. But I am grown up now, you know, and I think I should be out on my own. I don't feel I was cut out to be on a farm. In a city there are lots of opportunities to get ahead, so I want to go and try my luck there. I do hope you will understand."

To his amazement, his father was more understanding than he ever dreamed!

"Son," he said, "if you've really decided to leave home, I will not stand in your way. But I want you to remember that wherever you go and whatever you do, you will always be a member of our family, and I will always love you."

Then the father gave his son his share of his inheritance money. So it was that the son left home with the assurance of his father's love and a pocket full of money!

As it turned out, life in the big city proved to be quite different from what he expected.

To begin with, the rent for the place where he decided to live was twice as much as he thought it would be, and the owner demanded payment for three months in advance!

Also, he fell in with a group of fellows who, having found out he had lots of money, promptly helped him spend it.

"'We'll show you the 'hot spots,'" they said, and away they went to wild parties. There was no end to the things they found to amuse themselves, always expecting the son to pay the bills. Before long he was smoking and drinking with them and then using drugs!

For a while he thought he was having a good time, but, as his money kept disappearing, he began to wonder. The day he hit bottom was when the landlord ordered him out of his apartment for being behind in his rent.

He thought of turning to his friends. But one by one they had deserted him when they found his money was gone. He had told his father he wanted to be "on his own." That was where he was now. All alone!

"Maybe a farmer would hire me," he said to himself. So he rolled the few clothes he had left into a backpack and hitchhiked out of the city.

The man who picked him up on the highway turned out to be a farmer.

"Where are you going?" the farmer asked.

"Anywhere that I can find a job," the young man answered.

The farmer looked him over, then said, "I happen to need a man to feed my hogs. You can have that job if you want it."

"I'll take it!" he said.

Later, as he was feeding the hogs, he was so hungry that he was almost ready to eat some of the garbage they were eating.

"Back home it was never like this," he said to himself. "My father always saw to it that his servants had enough to eat and more. I'm going home!"

So the next day, he started for home!

In the meantime, back home his father was lonely and homesick for his youngest son, wondering where he was and how he was getting along, wishing he would write, and hoping he would come home. Every day he would go out on the front steps of his home and look far down the road, hoping to see him coming back. One day he did see a figure coming over the hill, a mile away. Could that be his son? He rushed into the house for his field glasses and back out again. Yes, it looked like him! His clothes were torn and badly worn and looked almost like rags! But he was sure it was his son. He could tell by the way he walked. Down the steps he went, two or three at a time, and on out into the road, running to meet him! Once they were face to face, his son held back, he was so ashamed. He looked like a tramp and smelled like the hogs. But his father threw his arms around his son. He hugged him and kissed him again and again! Tears rolled down the cheeks of both of them!

It was the son who spoke first. "Father," he said, "what I did was very wrong. I was thinking only of myself. I have sinned against God and against you! I am not worthy to be your son anymore. Won't you let me be one of your servants?"

Arm in arm they walked on up toward the house. Once in the yard, his father began calling to his servants.

To one he said, "Go to the closet and get the finest robe in the house. Bring it and put it on him." To another, "In my jewel box, find the finest ring. Bring it and put it on his finger!"

To still another, "Go to the pasture! Choose the fattest calf in the herd, kill it, dress it, and roast it for dinner. This very night we will have a feast in honor of my son. I was afraid he was dead, but see, he is alive and well!"

In short order the servants hurried

away to do as they had been commanded. It was to be a fun night—a big celebration, with everyone happy—and happiest of all the father because his son had come home!

At this point Jesus could have ended the story. But he did not. In this next part of the story, He was in effect saying to the Jewish religious leaders, "I have drawn a picture of God as a loving Father and how He feels toward lost sinners when they repent and come back home. Now I will draw *your* picture. You are like the son's older brother.

"When the brother came in from working in the field and heard merry music and saw all the servants hurrying here and there preparing food, he asked one of them what was going on.

"Before he could finish his question, the servant broke in, 'Your brother is back home again! And your father is so happy that he has ordered us to prepare a feast to celebrate his return!'

"At that, the older brother became jealous and began to pout, 'Well, I won't be there!' he said, and started to leave.

"Just then his father came out and begged him to come in. Still pouting, the older son said, 'Year after year I have stayed at home, helping with the work on the farm, doing whatever you asked me to do. And during all that time you never gave me so much as a little goat to have a party with my friends. But when this son of yours comes back from the big city where he wasted your money on wild parties, you celebrate by killing and roasting the fattest calf in the herd! Come to *his* feast? No, thank you!'

"'My dear boy,' his father answered, 'please don't act like that! You have always been and still are very dear to me,

and one of these days all that I have will belong to you. But I love my other son, too, and he is your brother. It is almost as if he had been dead or lost, and now has been found and is alive! Come in and be happy with us!'"

Did the older son change his attitude toward his brother and go in to welcome him? We are not told, but we hope he did, don't we?

Prayer:

Dear God, through this wonderful story
  of Jesus I hear You saying to me that
When I do right, You love me
With a love that makes You glad.
When I do wrong, You love me
With a love that makes You sad.
But, right or wrong, You always love me.
I do thank You for loving me as You do,
And ask You to make me strong and
  good and true.
Amen.

Questions for Discussion

1. Name the main characters in the story Jesus told.
2. What happened when the son arrived in the city?
3. When and why did he decide to leave the city?
4. Where did he go next and what job did he find?
5. Describe his feelings when he became homesick.
6. Describe what the father did when he saw his son coming home.
7. What should be our attitude toward those who sin?

CHAPTER TWENTY-TWO

OBEDIENCE – CHORE OR CHEER?

Do you sometimes help with the chores at home? Like washing or drying the dishes for your mother? Or helping your dad clean up the yard or wash the car?

And do you sometimes get paid for doing such things—like being given some money or a special treat or receiving a weekly allowance?

Are there other times when you do something helpful for your father and mother, on their birthday, for example, just because you love them, when you don't expect any kind of pay at all?

If so, which kind of helpfulness means most to them?

The last kind, of course! The kind in which you forget all about getting paid or even praised, when you think only of *giving happiness!*

Once Jesus told a story which teaches what means most to God. When we do something for Him, it is not how much we do, but the spirit in which we do it!

* * * * * * *

If He were telling the story today, it probably would go something like this:

Once there was a man who owned a large vineyard. As he walked through it late one afternoon, he realized that the time for harvesting his grapes had come. The grapes were ripe and should be picked at once.

So the next morning he got up early and drove down in his truck to the employment office in the city. Several men were sitting outside, obviously in need of a job. Walking up to them he said, "I have a large vineyard and my grapes are ready to be picked. Will you come and work for me today?"

One of the men asked, "How much will you pay us?"

"My friend," the vineyard owner replied, "my grapes are ripe and need to be picked today. I will pay each of you $25.00."

The men agreed and they climbed into his truck and he drove them to his vineyard. There the foreman in charge gave to each a large basket and instructions about picking the grapes.

At noon, the owner of the vineyard drove back to the employment office where he found another group waiting to be hired. After telling them who he was and his need to finish harvesting his grapes before they became overripe, he said, "If you will help me, at the end of the day I will pay you what is fair."

The men climbed into the truck and drove away with him to work in his vineyard.

Still later in the day, the vineyard owner drove back into town where he found several other men in front of the employment office.

To them he said, "The day is almost over, why are you not working?"

"No one has offered us a job," they replied.

75

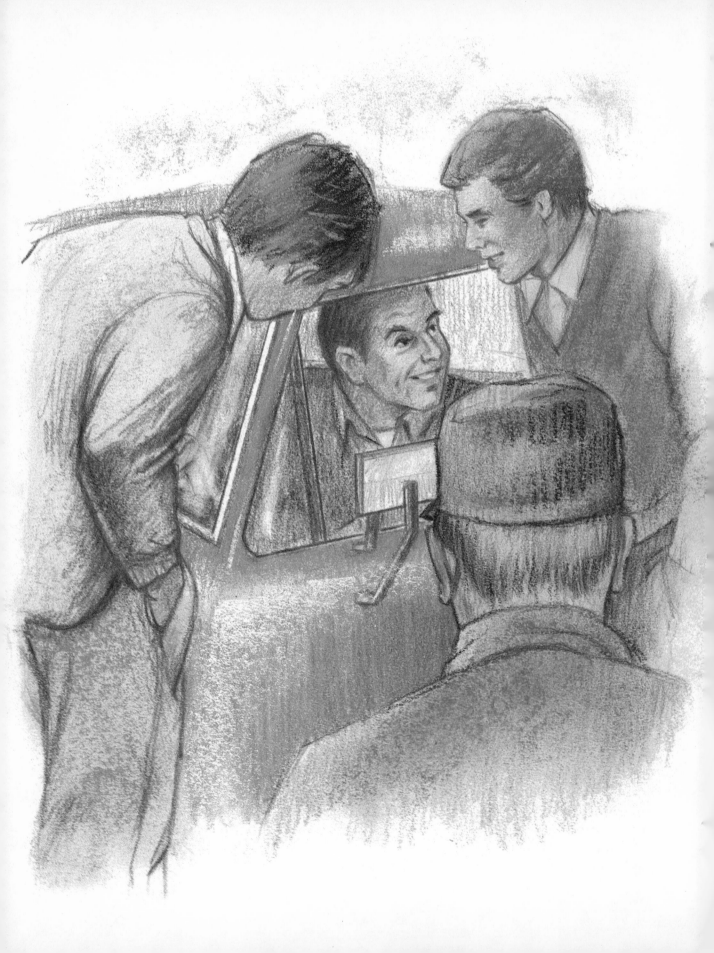

"Will you come help me finish harvesting my grapes?" asked the vineyard owner. "I will pay you what is fair."

So the third group of men went to work for the vineyard owner even though it was late in the day.

At the end of the day, the owner of the vineyard said to his foreman, "Call the workers together and pay them their wages."

All the workers were surprised when the group who had been hired last were given $25.00 each. The group who were hired first were not only surprised, but boiling mad when each of them received $25.00.

"We demand to see the owner of the vineyard!" they said.

So the vineyard owner came out and the men exploded, "What goes here? We worked in your vineyard all day, through the heat of the noonday sun, and you are paying us no more than you paid those you hired at five o'clock! Why is that?"

"Calm down, my friend," the vineyard owner answered in a quiet voice. "You agreed to work for $25.00 a day, and that is what you have been paid. If I choose to be generous to those who trusted me and were willing to work for me, is that any business of yours? Do I not have right to do what I will with what belongs to me? Are you envious because I am generous?"

And with that, he turned and walked away!

By this story we are taught that the spirit in which we serve God matters more to Him than how long we serve, or the amount of work we do. Therefore we should always try to serve Him, not only faithfully, but with glad and willing hearts.

Prayer:

Dear God,
> If, as Your Word says, You love the *cheerful giver,*
> Then You must love the *cheerful doer* too.
> So, teach me the secret of *happy* obedience,
> Teach me to do the things I should—at home, at school, in church—not from a sense of duty,
> But because I want to serve You.
> Each day may I serve You faithfully,
> With a glad and willing spirit.
Amen.

Questions for Discussion

1. In this story, describe the vineyard owner's conversation with the first group of men he found at the employment office.
2. What were the terms of the agreement under which they agreed to work?
3. Describe the vineyard owner's conversation with the second and third group.
4. What were the terms under which they agreed to work?
5. Why did the vineyard owner pay the last group as much as he did the first?
6. Why did the first group have no right to protest?
7. What kind of obedience is most pleasing to our parents? to our teachers? to God?

CHAPTER TWENTY-THREE

FORGIVENESS UNLIMITED

Do you sometimes find it hard to forgive a friend or a member of your family who did something or said something that hurt you and who did it more than once?

Apparently that was the kind of problem Peter was having. Perhaps his problem was with one of the disciples. Possibly it was with his own brother, Andrew. At any rate someone had done something to Peter and Peter had forgiven him.

But the very next day he had done the same thing again, and again he had apologized. But Peter was finding it hard to forgive him a second time.

So he turned to Jesus for help—which, of course, was a very wise thing to do!

"Master," he said, "if my brother sins against me, how many times am I expected to forgive him?" Then he paused. Two or three times came to his mind as a fair answer. But knowing how forgiving Jesus was to sinners who repented, and since to the Jews seven was considered a perfect number, he added, "Seven times?"

Peter was in for the surprise of his life! Because Jesus came back with the amazing answer, "No, not up to *seven* times, but up to *seventy times seven.*"

Now by that answer Jesus did not mean that Peter should stop forgiving at 490 times, which is seventy times seven. He meant that in considering and practicing forgiveness, Peter should not think in terms of numbers at all, but be ready and willing to forgive wherever and whenever he was asked to do so. In other words, that he should place no limit whatever upon his forgiveness!

Can't you imagine how stunned Peter was by that answer of Jesus? And can't you imagine him thinking, *But why should I or anyone be expected to forgive like that?*

While he did not speak that question, Jesus must have read his mind, because that is the very question Jesus proceeded to answer—only His answer was in the form of a story.

* * * * * * *

Had Jesus been telling the story today, it would probably go something like this.

Once there was a king who was very wealthy and who had made generous loans of money to several members of his court. The time drew near when the loans would be due, and the king sent out notices that on a certain day all loans were to be repaid.

The first man called in was his prime minister, whose debt with interest added in, amounted to ten million dollars! As it turned out, he was not able to pay and the king ordered all that he had to be sold and the money brought to him as payment on the debt.

The prime minister fell upon his knees before the king and pleaded, "Your Majesty, give me time to collect from those who owe me. I promise to pay my debt in full."

Now the king was a kind man. Taking the hand of his prime minister and lifting him to his feet he said, "Suppose, instead of giving you more time I tell you you don't owe me anything. Your debt is cancelled in full."

At this point in Jesus' story, the king represented God and how He forgives. The prime minister could hardly believe his ears! What he had heard sounded too good to be true! But it was true. His enormous debt of ten million dollars was no more. "From the bottom of my heart, I thank you Your Majesty," he said, and went home very happy!

But the next day, as he checked his own records he found a man who owed him two thousand dollars—a very small debt compared to his own huge debt which the king had cancelled the day before. The prime minister went to the man's house, knocked on his door, and when he opened it, grabbed him by the throat and said, "I want my two thousand dollars, and I want it now!"

Falling to his knees the man begged for a little time. "Be patient with me. Give me a month and I will pay every dollar I owe you."

But instead of treating him as he himself had been treated by the king, he had the man arrested and thrown in jail until the debt could be paid in full.

Now some of the man's friends reported to the king what had happened, and he lost no time in calling the prime minister to appear before him.

"You greedy, heartless wretch," he said. "I cancelled the ten million dollar debt you owed me. Why did you not show the same mercy toward the man who owed you only two thousand dollars?" And the king had the prime minister thrown into jail.

By this story, Jesus was teaching Peter, and through him is teaching us, that since God is so loving and forgiving toward us, we also ought to be loving and forgiving toward others.

Prayer:

Dear God,
Keep me from ever holding a grudge,
Or from keeping bitter thoughts in my mind.
Help me to treat others as I would have others treat me,
And to be always loving, unselfish, and kind.
Teach me to forgive, as You have forgiven me.
Amen.

Questions for Discussion

1. What was the question Peter asked Jesus?
2. What was Jesus' answer?
3. What did Jesus really mean by "seventy times seven?"
4. In the story Jesus told, what was the difference in the amount of money the two debtors owed?
5. In the story, who did the king represent when he forgave the ten million dollar debt?
6. What lesson did it teach Peter and us?